Identifying Chincoteague Ponies 2022

Cover photo: Fifteen Friends of Freckles with 2017 foal, Heide's Sky.

Other books from
Jennie's Music Room Books

Nicio and Cedar Fire
Legends of Two-Legs
Identifying Chincoteague Ponies [2017]
Identifying Chincoteague Ponies 2018
Identifying Chincoteague Ponies 2019
Identifying Chincoteague Ponies 2020
Identifying Chincoteague Ponies 2021

Jennie's Music Room Books
4241 Filmore St
Chincoteague Island, VA 23336

ISBN: 978-0-578-33214-7

Contents

Preface

About This Book

The primary purpose of this book is to aid in the identification of individual members of the feral herd of horses known as Chincoteague ponies. These ponies reside on the southern Virginia end of Assateague Island. There is a completely separate herd at the northern Maryland end of the island know as Assateague horses. The Maryland herd is not included in this book.

This book is the work of one person. The author took the photos, drew the drawings, created the video clips, collected the data, formatted the pages and published the book.

There will be times when you will not be able to positively identify an individual using one resource. Animals with solid coats and very light pintos can be hard to identify. Colors appear differently depending on the season, weather, and lighting conditions. Long hair in the winter may obscure brands. Mud can cover legs. Manes blow around.

The author recommends that when in doubt, search the internet. She starts with the Chincoteague Pony Pedigree Database at chincoteaguepedigrees.com. Besides interesting geneology information, there are links to other web sites with photo galleries and band information. Another method is to post pictures and ask in any of the various Facebook pony groups, like I Love Chincoteague Ponies!

To report errors or to make suggestions for next year's book, please message me through my Facebook page - Chincoteague Pony Names.

Organization

Ponies are grouped alphabetically by color. **Bay**: Any dark colored horse with black points*. Colors range from shades of red to very dark brown. **Black**: An all black horse including points*. **Buckskin**: Any light colored horse with black/brown points*. Colors range from very light cream to yellow, tan, or gold. **Chestnut**: A reddish brown horse. Colors range from light red to deep mahogany. **Palomino**: A pale horse with white mane and tail. Colors range from cream to golden.

*points: legs, muzzle, mane and tail, and tips of ears

Each color is divided into 3 sections. **Solid:** A horse with no white markings on the body other than face and legs. **Comparison Chart**: Additional characteristics that might aid in identifying a solid horse. **Pinto**: A horse with white markings on the body other than face and legs. Any horse could have white on the face and legs.

Alphabetical by name, brand, and stallion indexes are included. The alphabetical index includes official names and popular nicknames.

There is also an family index which shows the relationships of the current living members of the herd. For more detailed pedigrees, refer to the Chincoteague Pony Pedigree Database at chincoteaguepedigrees.com.

Bay Girl

Fluffy
mare   birth year: 1999   brand: none
WITCH DOCTOR x WILD ISLAND ORCHID

Brown eyes.

Video Clip

Pedigree

Notes:

Bay Girl

Bay

Daisey

mare   birth year: 2004   brand: none
Cinnamon Hologram x Merry Teapot's High Bid

Brown eyes. Sold at the 2004 auction and donated back to CVFD in 2012 by auction buyer Don Thornton. Alternate sire: Witch Doctor, Alternate dam: Wild Island Orchid.

Video Clip

Pedigree

Notes:

Daisey

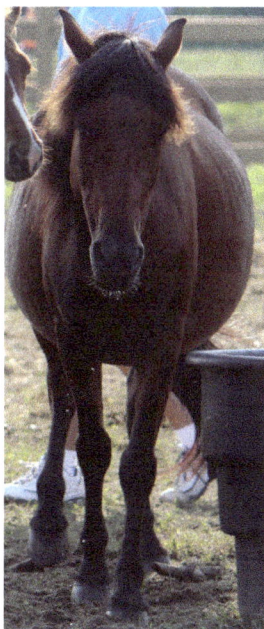

Doc's Bay Dream

Bay Dream
mare   birth year: 2018   brand: 18
Effie's Papa Bear x Doctor Amrien

Brown eyes. Auction price: $7,500. First seen April 5, 2018. Buyback donor: Dan and Abby Davis family, Darcy and Steve Cole, and friends of Capt Dan.

Video Clip

Pedigree

Notes:

_____

_____

_____

_____

_____

_____

_____

_____

Doc's Bay Dream

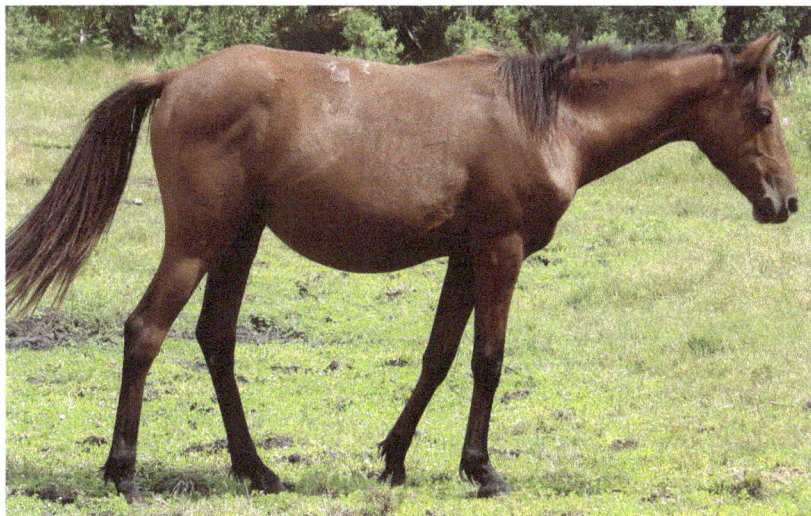

Bay

Effie's Papa Bear

Poseidon's Fury, Hoppy
stallion   birth year: 2007   brand: 07
SOCKETT TO ME x MERMAID

Brown eyes. Auction price: $7,500. Born April 9, 2007. Buyback donator: Stephanie Guerlain.

Video Clip

Pedigree

Notes:

Effie's Papa Bear

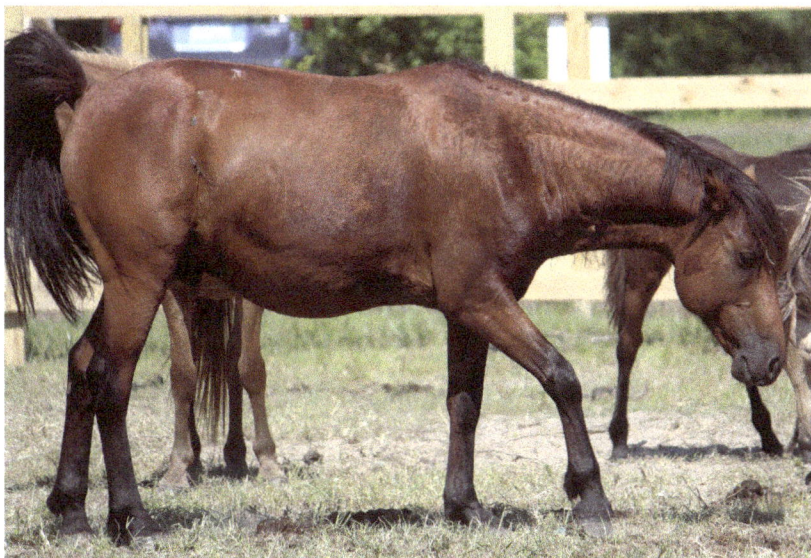

Bay

Little Dolphin

Neptune
stallion   birth year: 2008   brand: 08
RAINBOW WARRIOR x LANDRIE'S GEORGIA PEACH

Brown eyes. Born May 14, 2008. King Neptune. Donated back by raffle winner.

Video Clip

Pedigree

Notes:

Little Dolphin

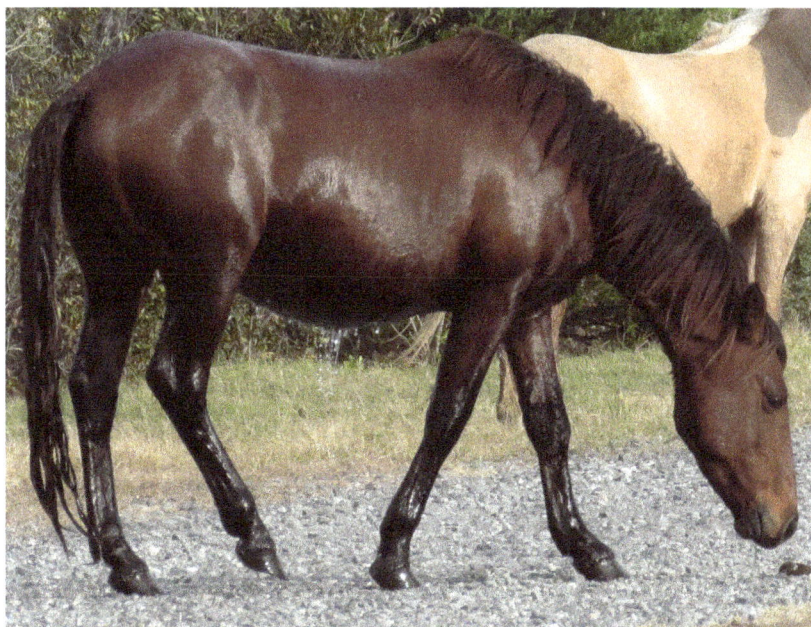

Bay

Pappy's Pony

mare   birth year: 2003   brand: 03
OCEAN STAR x ISLAND STAR

Brown eyes. Auction price: $6,600. Born July 16, 2003. Alternate sire: Witch Doctor. Buyback donor: Stepp family.

Video Clip   Pedigree

Notes:

Pappy's Pony

Bay

Pony Ladies' Sweet Surprise

Lady
mare   birth year: 2004   brand: 04
GUNNER'S MOON X SWEET INSPIRATION

Brown eyes. Auction price: $3,150. Born May 2, 2004. Buyback donor: Buyback Babes.

Video Clip   Pedigree

Notes:

_____

_____

_____

_____

_____

_____

_____

_____

Pony Ladies' Sweet Surprise

Bay

Thunderbolt

stallion   birth year: 2018   brand: 18
CHIEF GOLDEN EAGLE X BLING BLING

Brown eyes. First seen
May 14, 2018. Donated
back to CVFC.

Video Clip

Pedigree

Notes:

Thunderbolt

Bay

Two Teagues Taco

Taco
mare   birth year: 2005   brand: 05
Witch Doctor x Wild Island Orchid

Brown eyes. Auction price: $5,000. Born July 12, 2005. Buyback donator: Myfe Moore.

Video Clip

Pedigree

Notes:

Bay

Two Teagues Taco

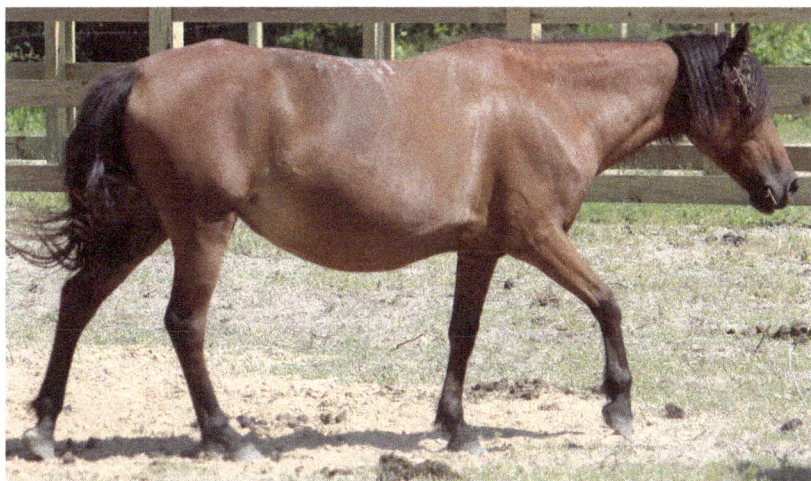

Jean Bonde's Bayside Angel

Angel
mare   birth year: 2015   brand: 15, partial
SOCKETT TO ME x LEAH'S BAYSIDE ANGEL

Brown eyes. Auction price: $6,400. Born April 22, 2015. Buyback donor: Buyback Babes.

Video Clip   Pedigree

Notes:

Jean Bonde's Bayside Angel

Bay

Leah's Bayside Angel

mare   birth year: 1999   brand: unreadable
OCEAN STAR x SUMMER BREEZE

Brown eyes. Born July 1999. Buyback donor: In memory of Leah Potter.

Video Clip   Pedigree

Notes:

Leah's Bayside Angel

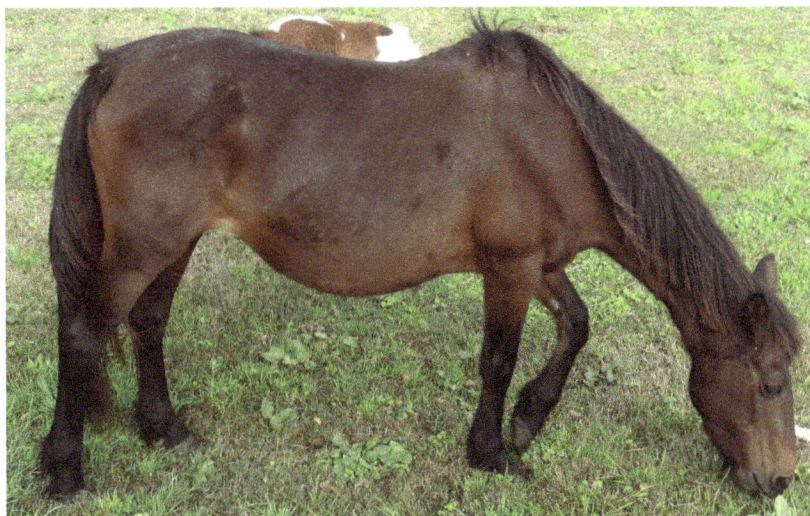

Bay

Tawny Treasure

mare   birth year: 2017   brand: 17
EFFIE'S PAPA BEAR x ISLE TREASURE

Brown eyes. Auction price: $7,100. First seen June 14, 2017. Buyback donator: Wanda and George Panos.

Video Clip   Pedigree

Notes:

Tawny Treasure

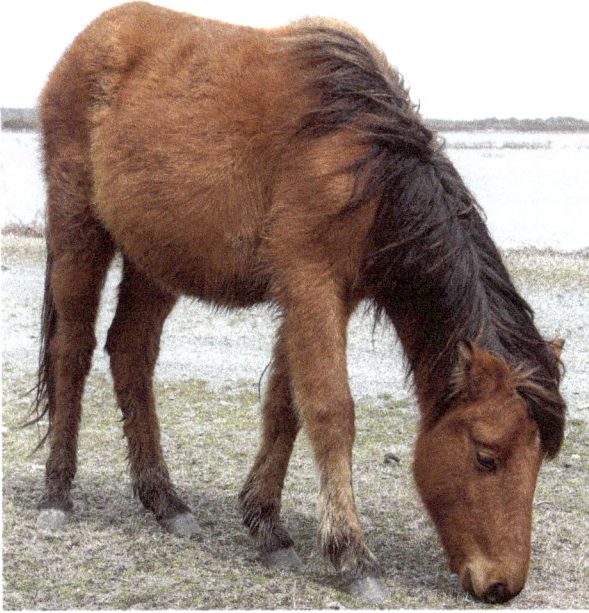

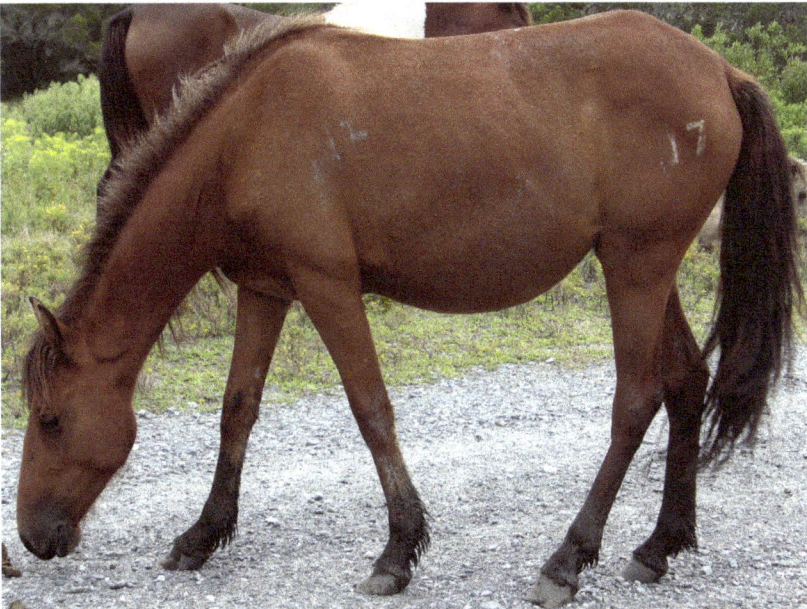

Bay

Dakota Sky's Cody Two Socks

Cody

mare   birth year: 2005   brand: 05, partial

COPPER MOOSE x STEVENSON'S DAKOTA SKY

Brown eyes. Auction price: $5,000. Born May 28, 2005. Buyback donor: Catherine Young.

Video Clip   Pedigree

Notes:

28

Dakota Sky's Cody Two Socks

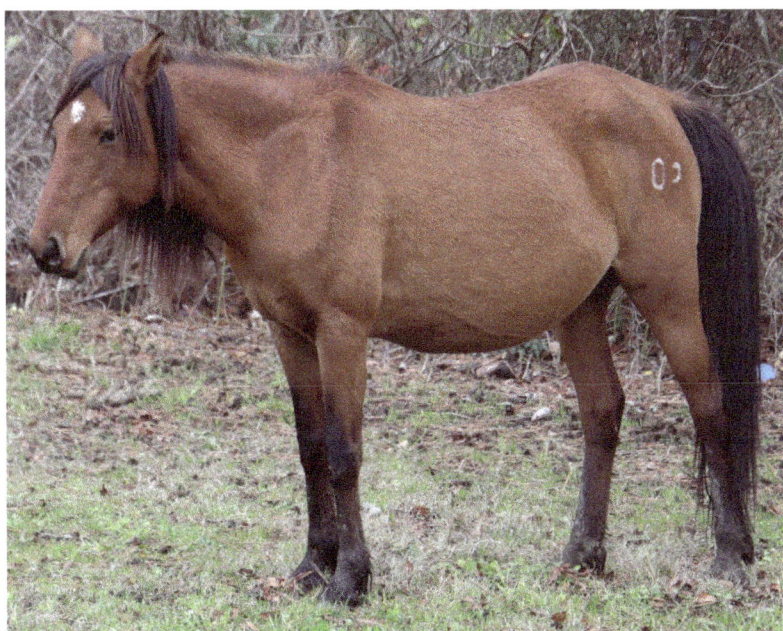

Bay Comparison Chart

Name	Pg #	Brand	Mane	Face	
Bay Girl	4		left		
Daisey	6		right		
Dakota Sky's Cody Two Socks	28	05, partial	right	star	
Doc's Bay Dream	8	18	left		
Effie's Papa Bear	10	07	left		
Jean Bonde's Bayside Angel	22	15, partial	left	star	
Leah's Bayside Angel	24	unreadable	right	star	
Little Dolphin	12	08	right		
Pappy's Pony	14	03	right		
Pony Ladies' Sweet Surprise	16	04	left		
Tawny Treasure	26	17	right	star	
Thunderbolt	18	18	right		
Two Teagues Taco	20	05	left		

NOTES

Left & right refers to the animal's left & right.

Mane: left = falls to the left **right** = falls to the right **split** = significant portion falls on left and right

Bay Comparison Chart

Legs				Notable Details
R F	R B	L F	L B	
	sock		sock	upper half of 5 is gone
				stallion; very dark mane and tail
				top of 1 in brand is obscured
				stallion; small statute
				stallion; 8 looks like a 0

R F = right front   **R B** = right back   **L F** = left front   **L B** = left back
sock = white well below the knee   **stocking** = white near and above the knee

baldface = white covers most of the face   **blaze** = white streak running down the length of the face   **snip** = white spot on the muzzle   **star** = white spot on the forehead

31

Bay Pinto

Rosie's Teapot

mare   birth year: 2013   brand: 13
AJAX x MOLLY'S ROSEBUD

Brown eyes. Born Fall 2013.

 Video Clip    Pedigree

Notes:

Rosie's Teapot

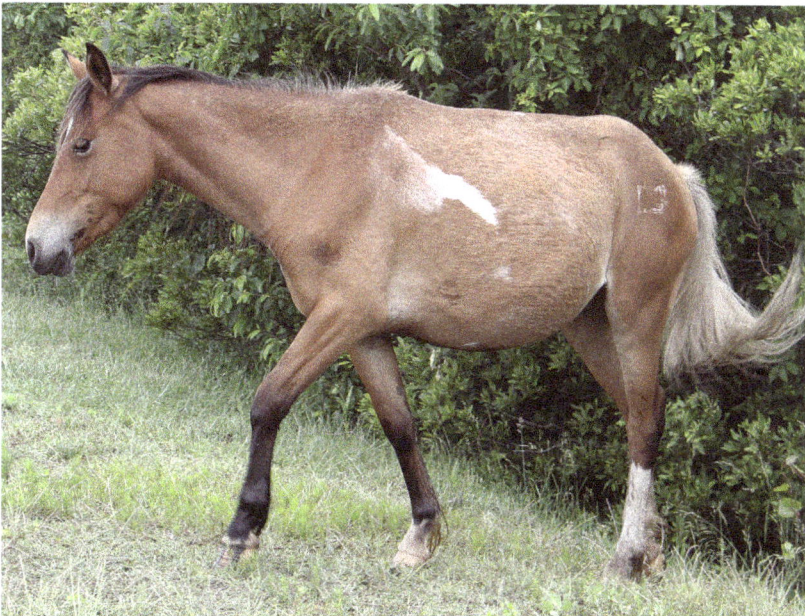

Bay Pinto

Raindancer's Shadow of Katet

Katet
mare   birth year: 2020   brand: 20
Archer's Gambit x Destiny Feathering Spirit

Brown eyes. First seen
April 22, 2020. Buyback
donor: Joanne Rome,
Ginny Zelevitch, Carol
Gazunis, and Olivia
Wheatley.

Video Clip

Pedigree

Notes:

Bay Pinto

Raindancer's Shadow of Katet

Bay Pinto

Scarlett's Little Bee

Little Bee, Bee
mare   birth year: 2019   brand: 19
KEN x MAY'S GRAND SLAM

Brown eyes. Auction price: $10,000. First seen June 23, 2019. Alternate sire: Archer's Gambit. Buyback donor: Debra Evalds.

Video Clip

Pedigree

Notes:

Scarlett's Little Bee

Bay Pinto

Good Golly Miss Molly

Molly
mare   birth year: 2019   brand: 19
TORNADO'S LEGACY x A SPLASH OF FRECKLES

Brown eyes. Auction price: $7,400. First seen May 27, 2019.

Video Clip

Pedigree

Notes:

Good Golly Miss Molly

Bay Pinto

Summer Breeze

Cee Cee, Breezy
mare   birth year: 2006   brand: none
Miracle Man x Binky's Breeze

Brown eyes. Born August 2006.

Video Clip

Pedigree

Notes:

_____

_____

_____

_____

_____

_____

_____

_____

Summer Breeze

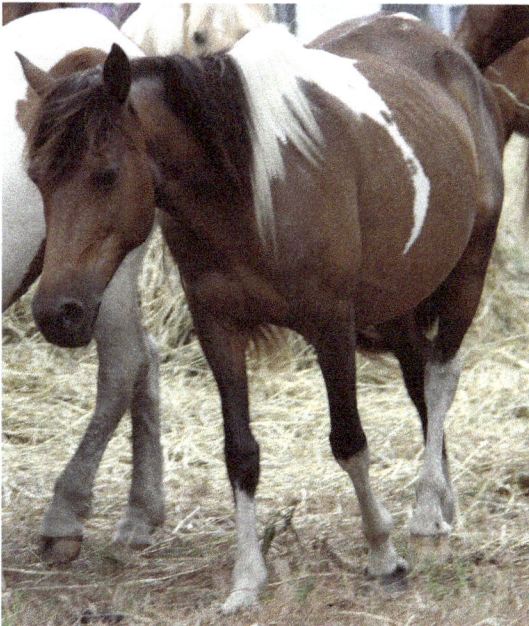

Bay Pinto

Amari's Journey

Journey
mare   birth year: 2020   brand: 20, partial
DON LEONARD STUD II x RANDY

Brown eyes. Auction price: $11,600. First seen May 14, 2020. Buyback donor: Dawn and Michael Feindt.

Video Clip   Pedigree

Notes:

Amari's Journey

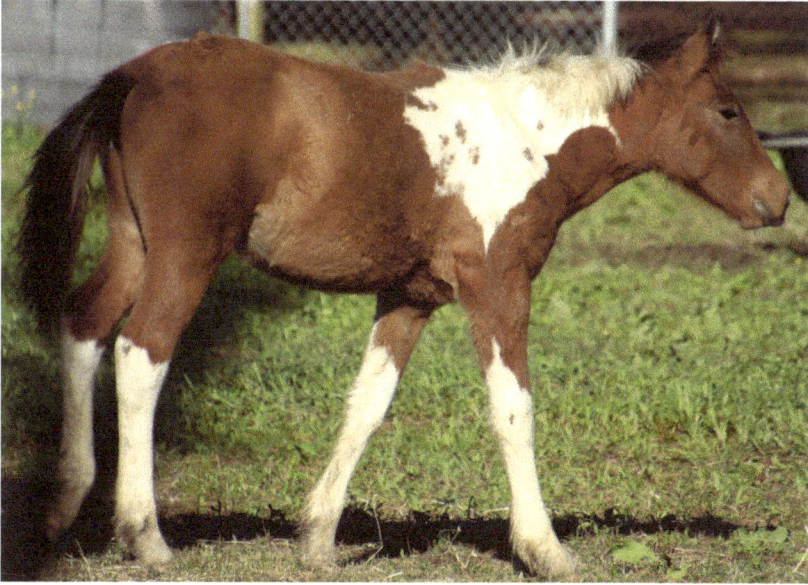

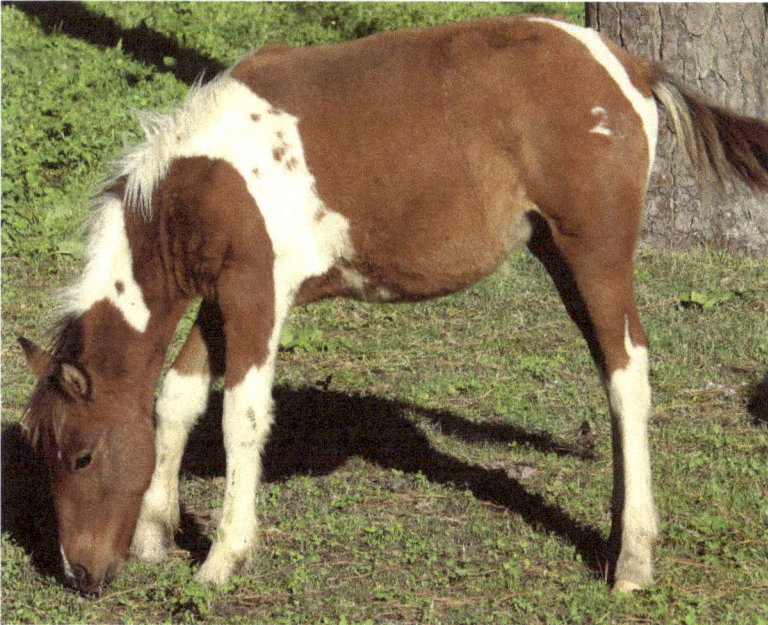

43

Bay Pinto

Ella of Assateague

Ella
mare   birth year: 2000   brand: 00
Cinnamon Hologram x Foxy Asset

Brown eyes. Born July 2000. Buyback donor: Cara Rosenbaum.

Video Clip   Pedigree

Notes:

Ella of Assateague

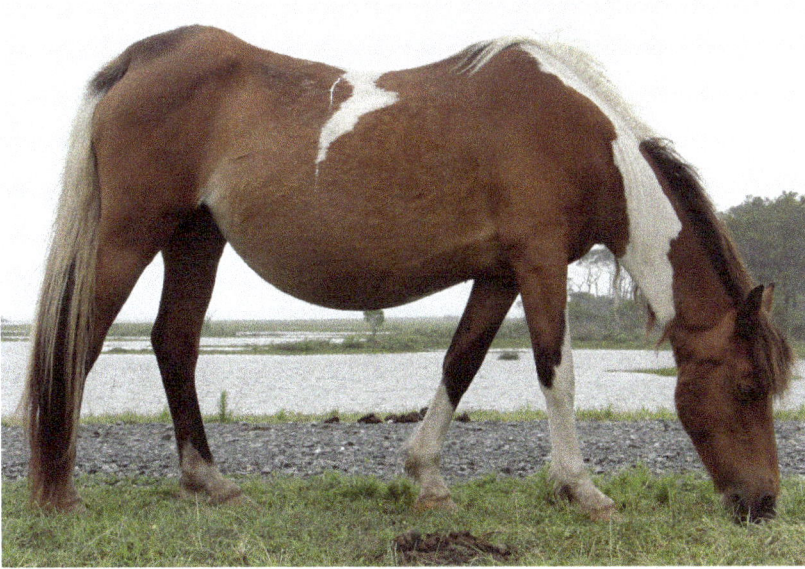

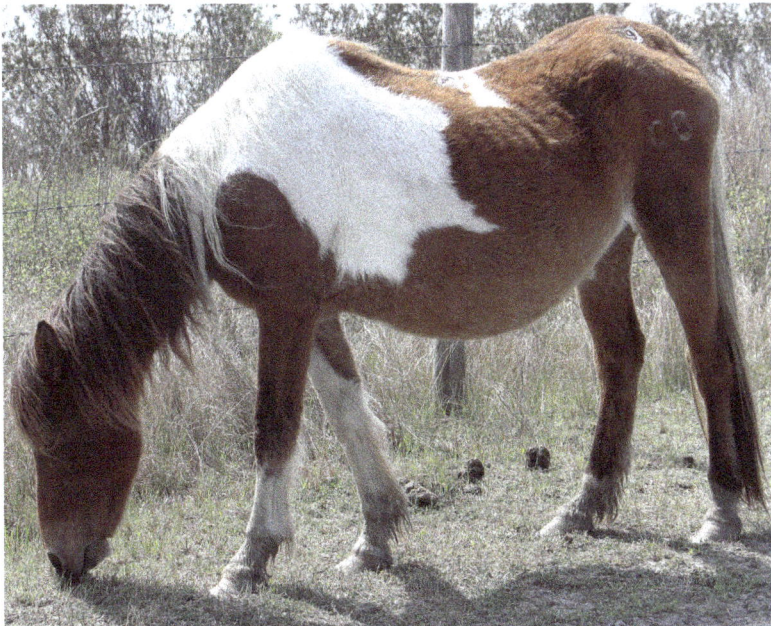

Bay Pinto

Billy Maez Renegade

Maezie
mare   birth year: 2020   brand: 20
ARCHER'S GAMBIT x SCOTTY ET

Brown eyes. Auction price: $13,100. First seen April 3, 2020. Buyback donor: Steph and Kevin Neyer.

Video Clip

Pedigree

Notes:

Billy Maez Renegade

Bay Pinto

Doctor Amrien

Doc
mare   birth year: 2014   brand: 14
Wild Thing x Dakota Sky's Cody Two Socks

Brown eyes. Born
September 1, 2014.
Buyback donor: Dan
and Abby Davis family.

Video Clip

Pedigree

Notes:

Bay Pinto

Doctor Amrien

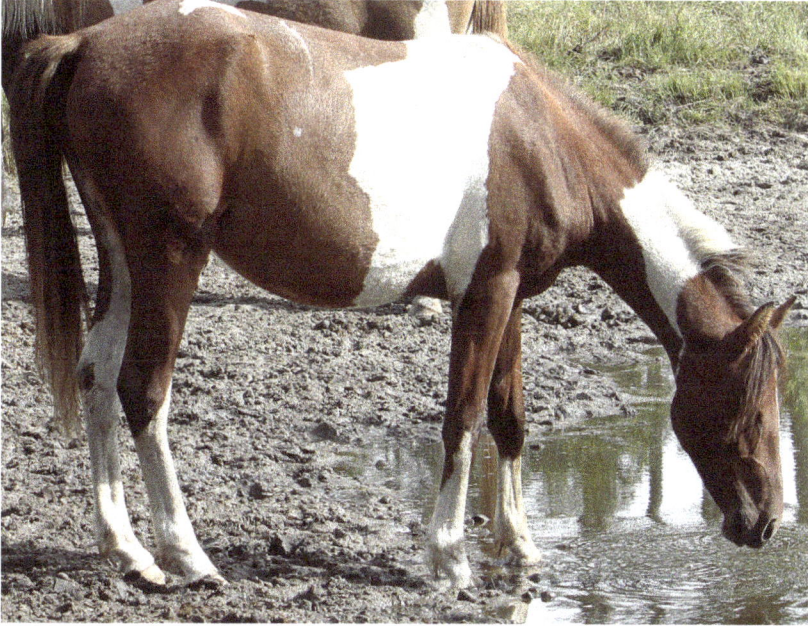

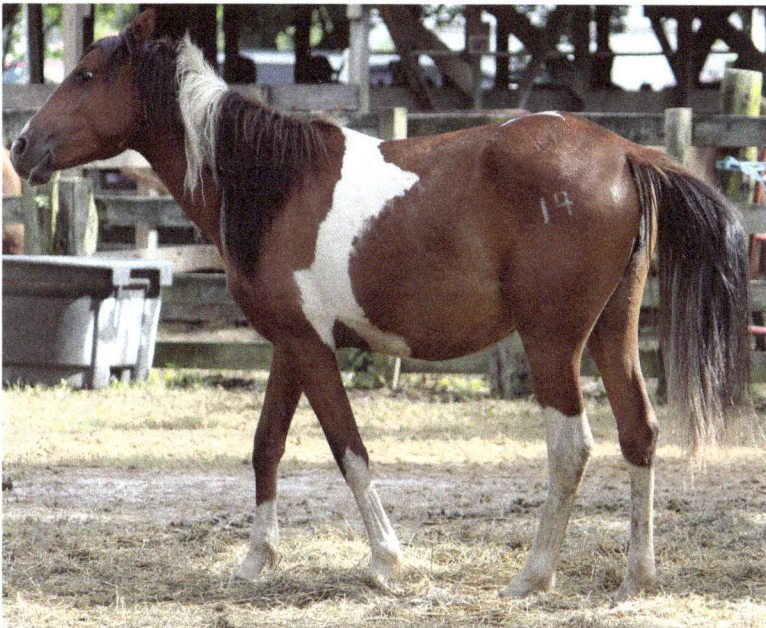

Bay Pinto

White Saddle

mare   birth year: 2013   brand: 13
WITCH DOCTOR x WILD ISLAND ORCHID

Brown eyes. Auction price: $4,100. Born April 5, 2013. Buyback donator: Joan Bradley.

Video Clip

Pedigree

Notes:

White Saddle

Bay Pinto

Miracle's Natural Beauty

Natural Beauty
mare   birth year: 2009   brand: 09
MIRACLE MAN x NATURAL INNOCENCE

Brown eyes. Auction price: $3,100. Born April 30, 2009. Buyback donator: Debbie and Landrie Folsom.

Video Clip

Pedigree

Notes:

Miracle's Natural Beauty

Bay Pinto

May's Grand Slam

May
mare   birth year: 2012   brand: 12
MIRACLE MAN x SPANISH ANGEL

Brown eyes. Auction price: $4,700. Born April 23, 2012. Buyback donator: Loveland family.

Video Clip

Pedigree

Notes:

May's Grand Slam

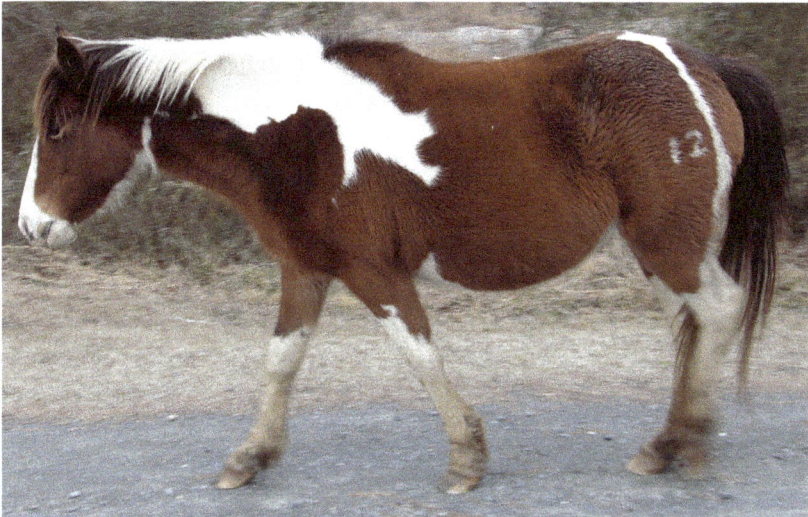

Bay Pinto

Tunie

Queenie
mare   birth year: 2003   brand: 03
WILLIE'S MAJESTIC DREAMER X SEASIDE

Brown eyes. Born
July 7, 2003. Queen
Neptune. Donated back
by raffle winner.

Video Clip

Pedigree

Notes:

Bay Pinto

Tunie

Bay Pinto

Wendy's Carolina Girl

Carolina Girl
mare   birth year: 2018   brand: 18
MAVERICK x ESSIE

Brown eyes. Auction price: $6,500. First seen May 14, 2018. Buyback donator: Wendy Sloan.

Notes:

Wendy's Carolina Girl

Bay Pinto

Ajax

stallion   birth year: 2007   brand: 07, partial
YANKEE SPIRIT x FOXY ASSET

Brown eyes. Auction price: $6,600. Born April 6, 2007. Buyback donor: Cara Rosenbaum.

Video Clip   Pedigree

Notes:

Ajax

Bay Pinto

MissMe

mare   birth year: 2017   brand: 17
AJAX x MIRACLE'S NATURAL BEAUTY

Brown eyes. Auction price: $13,500. First seen May 19, 2017. Buyback donor: Sydney Moore.

Notes:

MissMe

Bay Pinto

Norman Rockwell Giddings

Norm, Rocky
stallion   birth year: 2018   brand: none
ARCHER'S GAMBIT X BABE

Brown eyes. Auction price: $4,000. First seen May 1, 2018. Donated to the CVFC October 2019. Tested homozygous for tobiano.

Video Clip

Pedigree

Notes:

Norman Rockwell Giddings

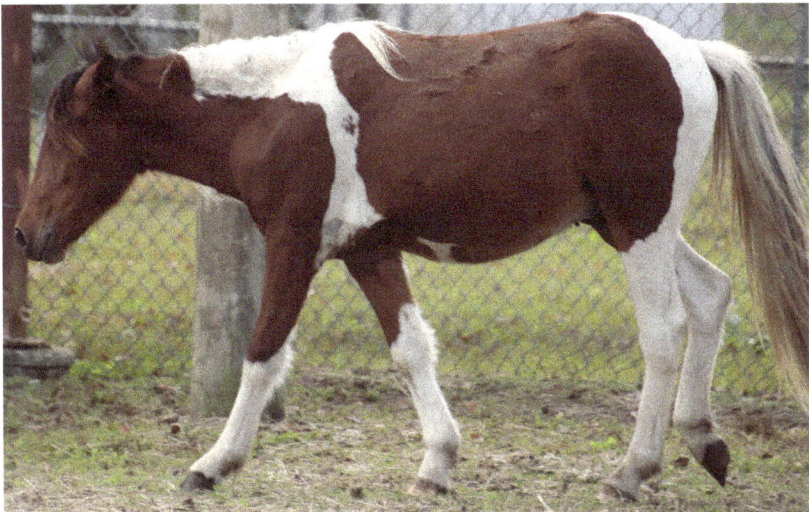

Bay Pinto

Destiny Feathering Spirit

Destiny
mare   birth year: 2002   brand: none
Courtney's Boy x Vixen

Brown eyes. Born
August 2002. Buyback
donor: Joann Rome
and Ginny Zlevitch.

Video Clip   Pedigree

Notes:

66

Destiny Feathering Spirit

Bay Pinto

Sweetheart

mare   birth year: 2011   brand: unreadable
WILD BILL x SCOTTY ET

Brown eyes. Auction price: $4,650. Born April 18, 2011. Buyback donator: Patty.

Video Clip

Pedigree

Notes:

Sweetheart

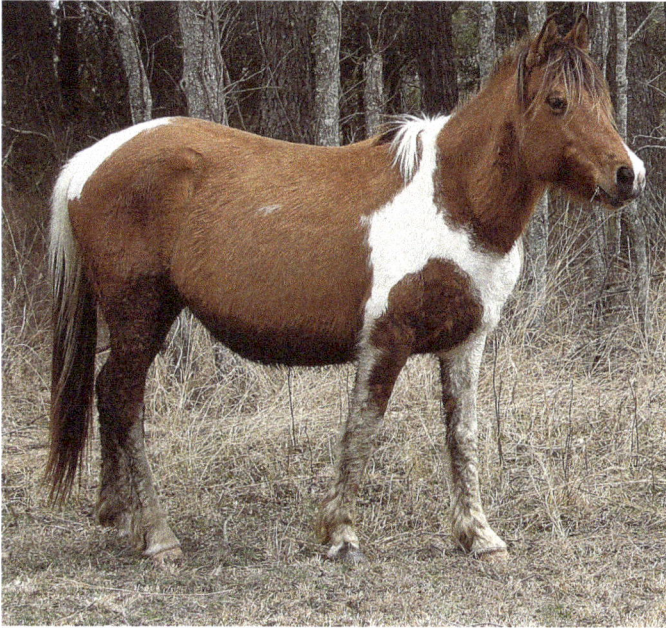

Bay Pinto

Henry's Hidalgo

stallion   birth year: 2017   brand: 17
WILD THING X THETIS

Brown eyes. Auction price: $8,900. First seen May 14, 2017. Buyback donor: Arthur Leonard.

Video Clip

Pedigree

Notes:

Henry's Hidalgo

Bay Pinto

Captain Carlton's Martha Lou

Martha Lou
mare   birth year: 2021   brand: 21
EFFIE'S PAPA BEAR x MARY READ

Brown eyes. Auction price: $10,600. First seen May 9, 2021. Buyback donor: In memory of Carlton Leonard.

Video Clip

Pedigree

Notes:

Captain Carlton's Martha Lou

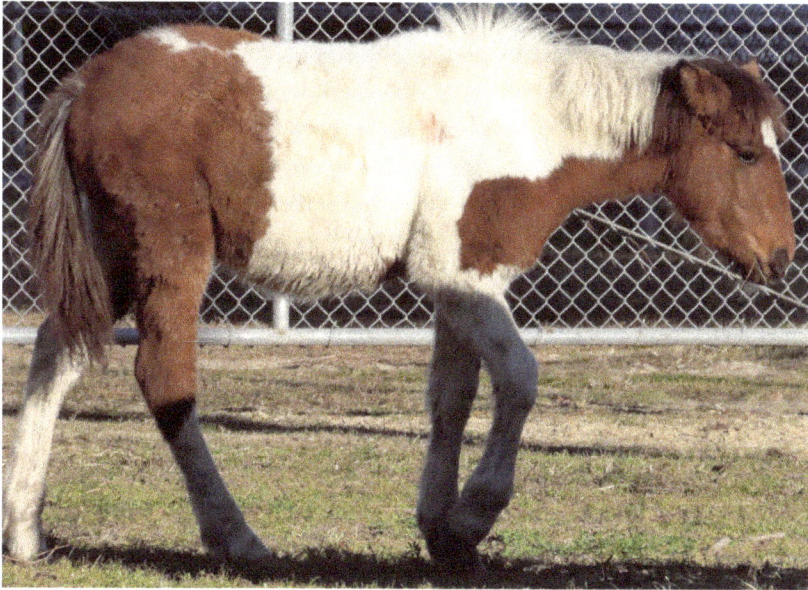

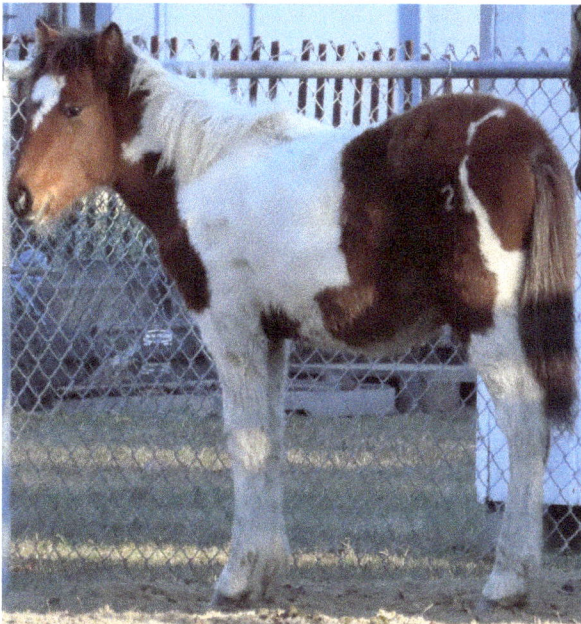

Bay Pinto

Splash

Danny's Girl
mare   birth year: 2014   brand: 14
WILD THING x SUMMER BREEZE

Brown eyes. Auction
price: $7,100. Buyback
donator: Beer Family.

Video Clip

Pedigree

Notes:

Splash

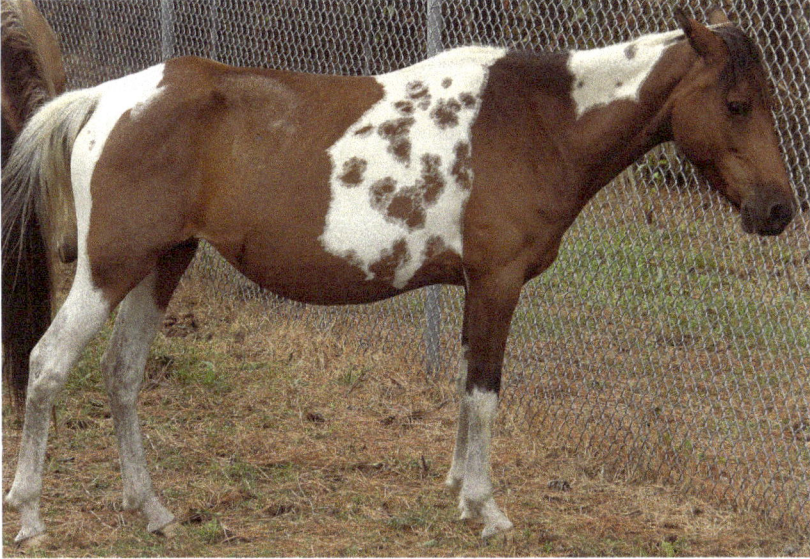

Bay Pinto

Beau of Artemis

Artemis
mare   birth year: 2021   brand: 21
WILD THING x THETIS

Brown eyes. Auction price: $23,000. First seen May 17, 2021. Buyback donor: Lori Basch, Hannon River, Jen Bush, Darcy Cole, Alison Dotzel, Tipson Myers.

Video Clip   Pedigree

Notes:

Beau of Artemis

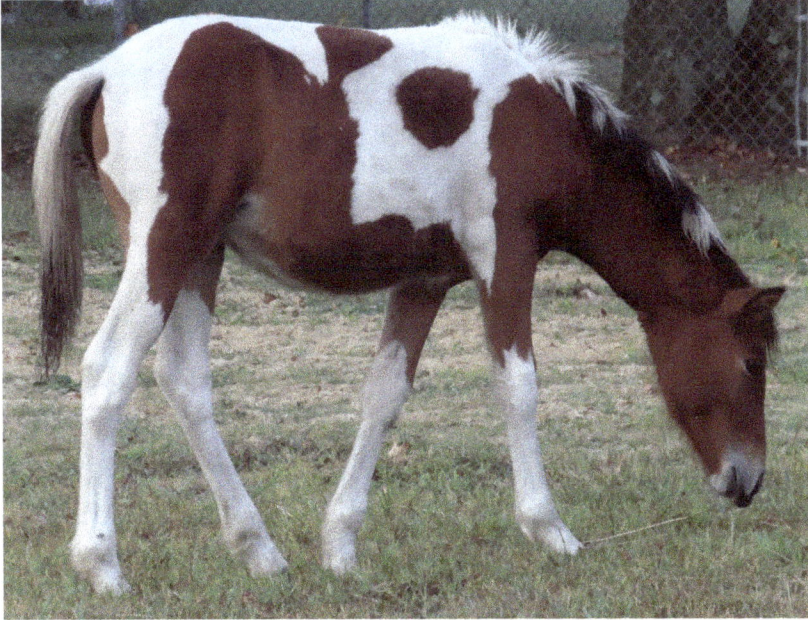

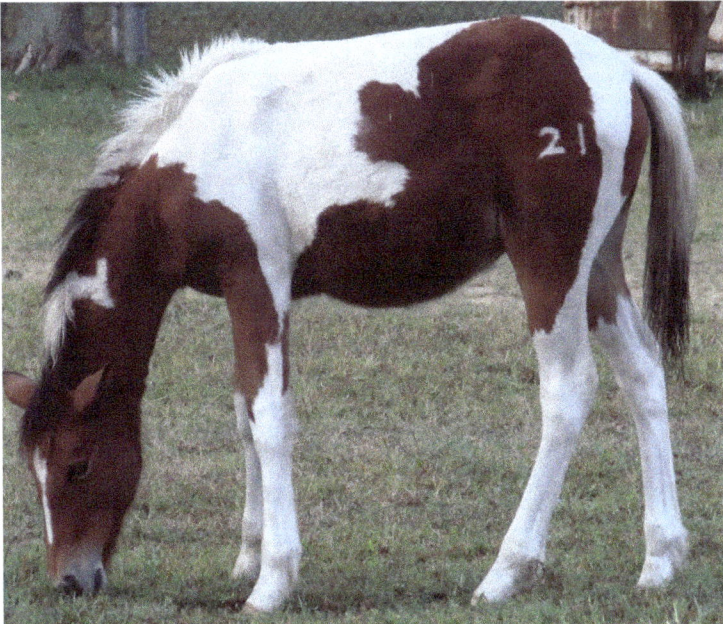

Bay Pinto

Grandma's Dream

mare   birth year: 2013   brand: 13
WILD THING x GALADRIEL

Brown eyes. Auction price: $4,600. Born May 7, 2013. Buyback donator: Frances Bidoglio.

Video Clip   Pedigree

Notes:

Grandma's Dream

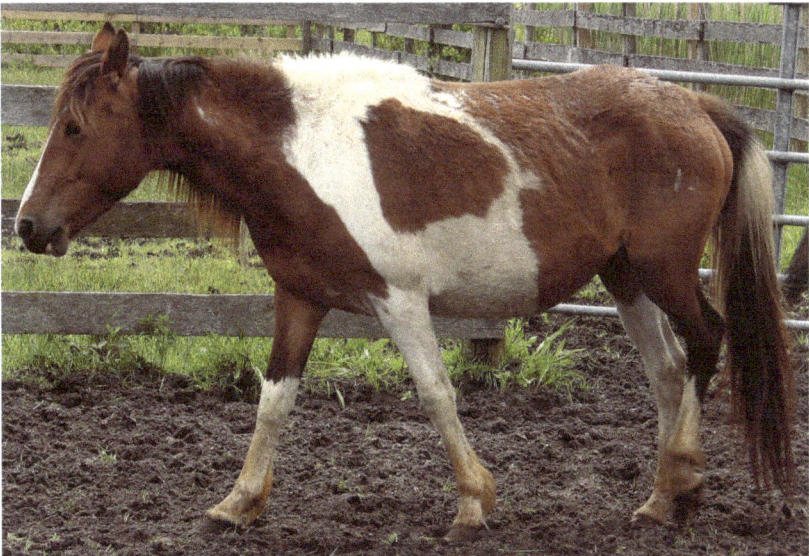

Bay Pinto

Loveland's Secret Feather

Secret, Feather
mare   birth year: 2012   brand: 12
WILD THING x GALADRIEL

Brown eyes. Auction price: $7,200. Born May 1, 2012. Buyback donator: Loveland family.

Video Clip   Pedigree

Notes:

Loveland's Secret Feather

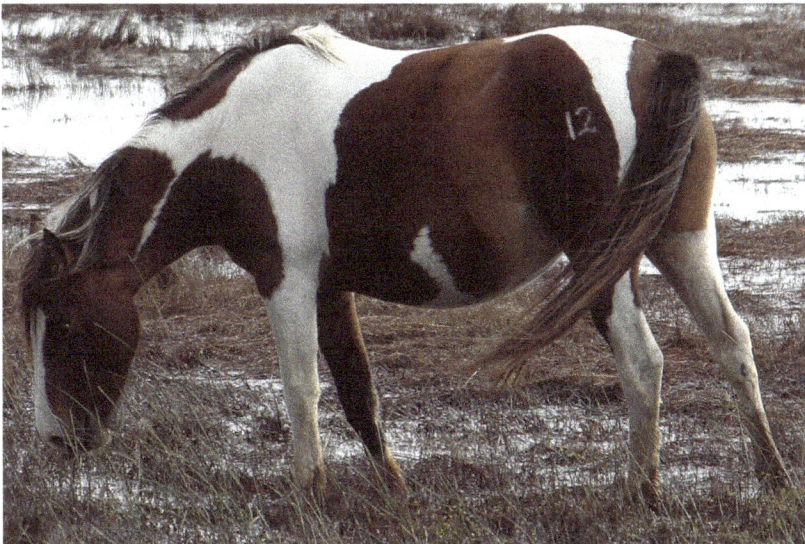

Bay Pinto

Wild Thing

stallion   birth year: 1997   brand: none
HURRICANE x JUST MY STYLE

Brown eyes.

Notes:

Wild Thing

Bay Pinto

Chickadee

mare   birth year: 2013   brand: 13
Courtney's Boy x Black Star

Brown eyes. Auction price: $5,000. Born April 15, 2013. Buyback donor: Janey Beer.

Video Clip   Pedigree

Notes:

Chickadee

Bay Pinto

Wildest Dreams

mare   birth year: 2008   brand: 08
MIRACLE MAN x NATURAL INNOCENCE

Brown eyes. Auction price: $7,200. Born April 28, 2008.

Video Clip

Pedigree

Notes:

Wildest Dreams

Bay Pinto

Marguerite of Chincoteague

mare   birth year: 2013   brand: 13
Tornado's Legacy x Miracle's Natural Beauty

Brown eyes. Auction price: $5,800. Born April 25, 2013. Alternate sire: Archer's Gambit. Buyback donator: Ellen Wycoski.

Video Clip   Pedigree

Notes:

Marguerite of Chincoteague

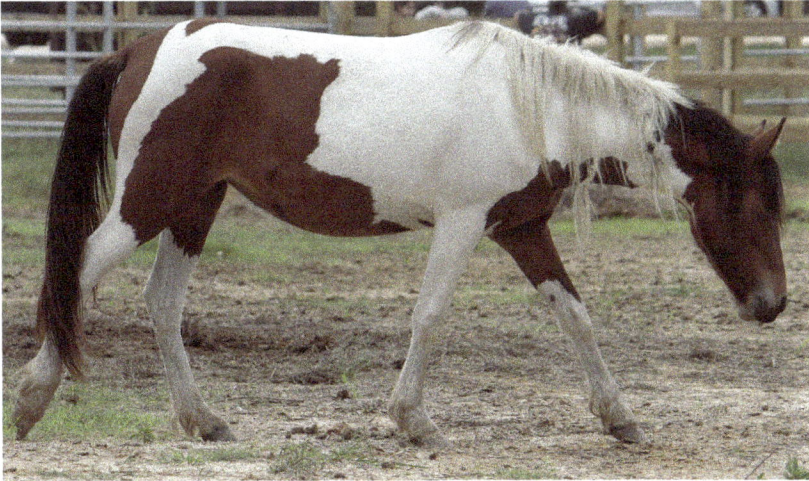

Bay Pinto

Shy Anne

Half n Half
mare   birth year: 1999   brand: none
HOT AIR BALLOON x SUNSHINE

Brown eyes. Born July 1999. Buyback donor: McCaskill family.

Video Clip

Pedigree

Notes:

Shy Anne

Bay Pinto

Fifteen Friends of Freckles

Freckles
mare   birth year: 2006   brand: 06
NORTH STAR x LZS MARK'S ISLAND LIBERTY

One blue, one brown eye. Auction price: $7,500. Born May 15, 2006. Buyback donor: Buyback Babes.

Video Clip

Pedigree

Notes:

Fifteen Friends of Freckles

Bay Pinto

Skylark

mare   birth year: 2011   brand: none
WILD THING x FOXY ASSET

Brown eyes. Auction
price: $4,000. Born
May 24, 2011. Buyback
donator: Kathleen
Cahall.

Video Clip

Pedigree

Notes:

Skylark

Bay Pinto

Scotty ET

ET
mare   birth year: 2002   brand: 02, partial
A<small>TTITUDE</small> x B<small>LACK</small> S<small>TAR</small>

Brown eyes. Auction price: $4,300. Born May 5, 2002. Buyback donor: Jean Bonde.

Video Clip

Pedigree

Notes:

Scotty ET

Bay Pinto

Winter Moon

Moon
mare   birth year: 2012   brand: none
CYCLONE II x HEART OF THE BAY

One blue, one brown eye. Born January 12, 2012. Donated to CVFC March 2018. Great great great grandfoal of Misty.

Video Clip   Pedigree

Notes:

Winter Moon

Bay Pinto

Sky Dancer

mare   birth year: 2019   brand: 19
AJAX x SKYLARK

Blue eyes. Auction price: $6,400. First seen July 13, 2019. Buyback donor: Liane Pfeiffer.

Video Clip

Pedigree

Notes:

Sky Dancer

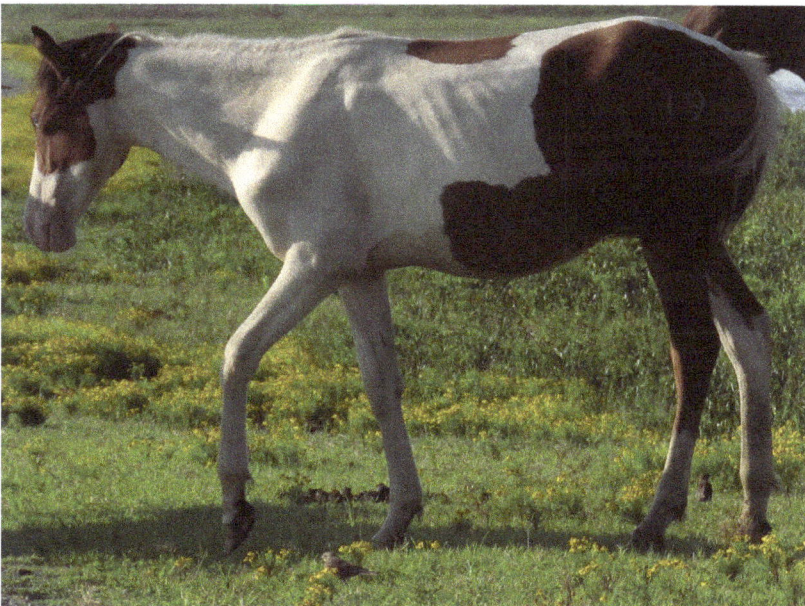

Bay Pinto

Summer

mare   birth year: 2015   brand: none
WH Nightwind x Justa Kickamazoo

Brown eyes. Donated to the CVFC March 2018. Great Great Great Grandfoal of Misty.

Video Clip   Pedigree

Notes:

Summer

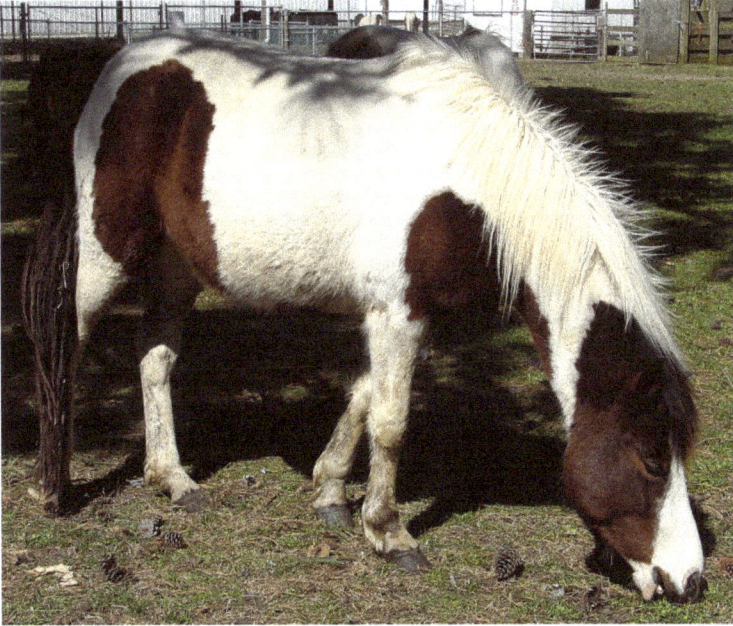

Bay Pinto

Seaside Miracle

mare   birth year: 2011   brand: F

Miracle Man x Seaside

Brown eyes. Auction price: $4,600. Born May 7, 2011.

Video Clip

Pedigree

Notes:

Seaside Miracle

Bay Pinto

A Splash of Freckles

Splash of Freckles
mare   birth year: 2011   brand: unreadable
NORTH STAR x FIFTEEN FRIENDS OF FRECKLES

Brown eyes. Auction price: $6,700. Born June 25, 2011. Buyback donor: Buyback Babes.

Video Clip   **Pedigree**

Notes:

A Splash of Freckles

Bay Pinto

Maverick

stallion   birth year: 2013   brand: 14
WILD THING x WITCH KRAFT

Brown eyes. Auction price: $12,700. Buyback donator: Catherine Miller. Born December 2013, sold at 2014 auction.

Video Clip

Pedigree

Notes:

Maverick

Bay Pinto

Got Milk

Anna
mare   birth year: 2000   brand: none
WITCH DOCTOR x WATERKOLOR

Brown eyes. Born October 8, 2000. Alternate sire: Top Gun.

Video Clip

Pedigree

Notes:

Got Milk

Bay Pinto

Heide's Sky

mare   birth year: 2017   brand: none

Ken x Fifteen Friends of Freckles

Blue eyes. First seen August 21, 2017. Buyback donor: Cindy Wolfe.

Video Clip

Pedigree

Notes:

Heide's Sky

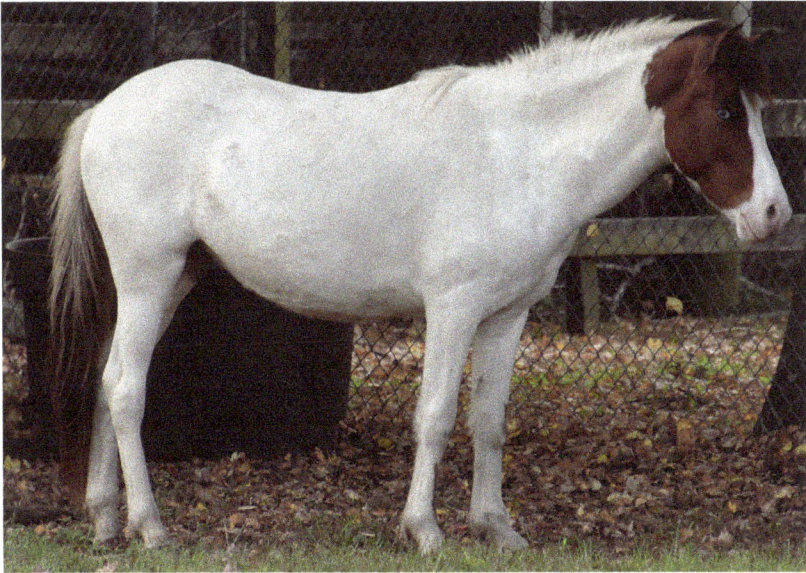

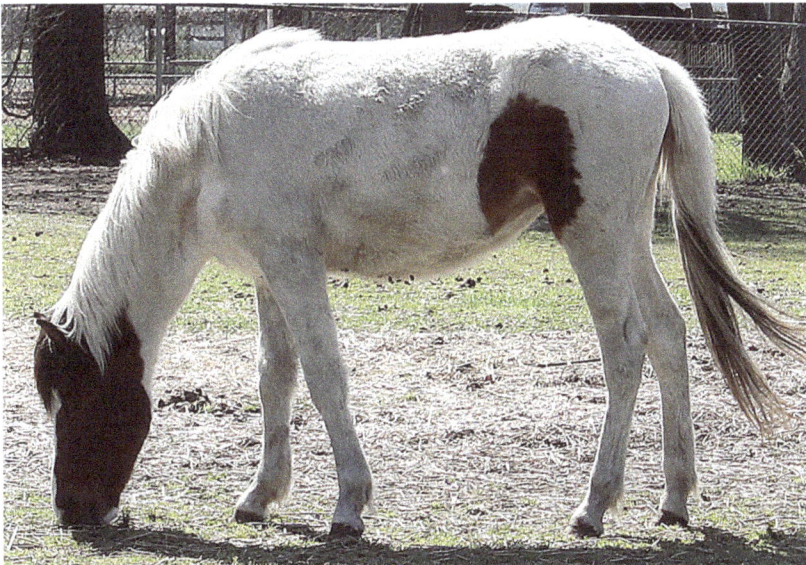

Black

CLG Ember

Ember
mare   birth year: 2018   brand: 18
SURFER'S RIPTIDE X BLACK PEARL

Brown eyes. Auction price: $11,000. First seen April 29, 2018. Buyback donor: Chincoteague Legacy Group.

Video Clip

Pedigree

Notes:

Black

CLG Ember

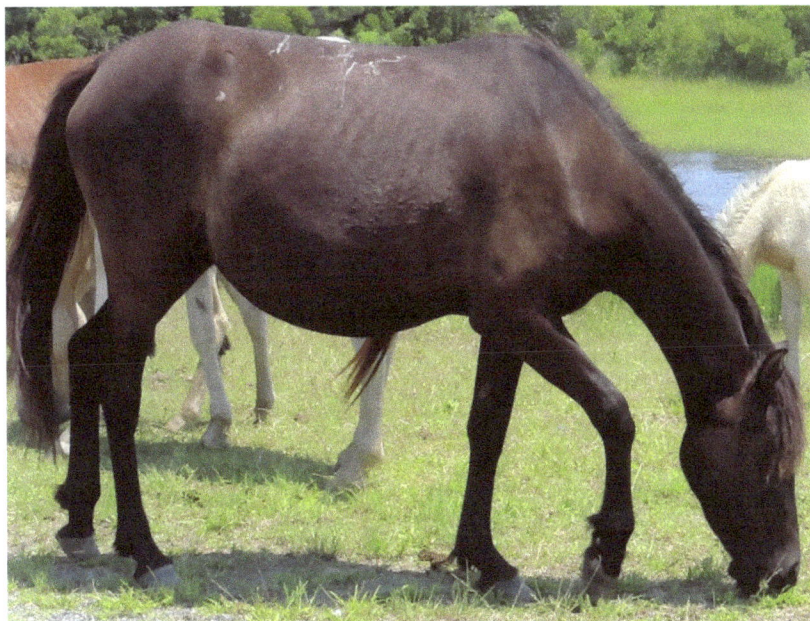

115

Black

Dexter's Midnight Runner

Dexie
mare   birth year: 2019   brand: 19
MAVERICK x BLACK PEARL

Brown eyes. Auction price: $17,500. First seen June 5, 2019.

Video Clip

Pedigree

Notes:

Dexter's Midnight Runner

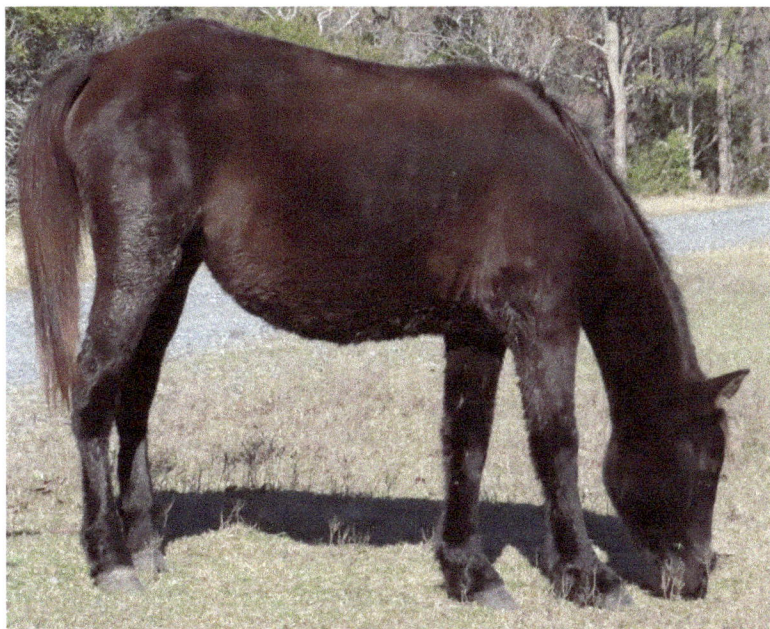

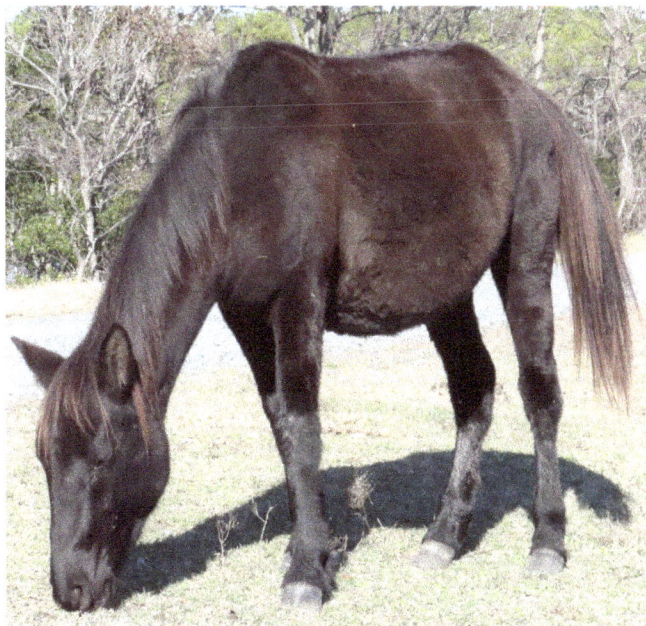

Black

Talia/Evan's Angel

Evan's Angel, Talia
mare   birth year: 2017   brand: 17
Maverick x Surfin' Chantel

Brown eyes. Auction price: $7,400. First seen May 21, 2017. Buyback donor: Greg and Lissa St. Claire.

Video Clip

Pedigree

Notes:

_____

_____

_____

_____

_____

_____

_____

Talia/Evan's Angel

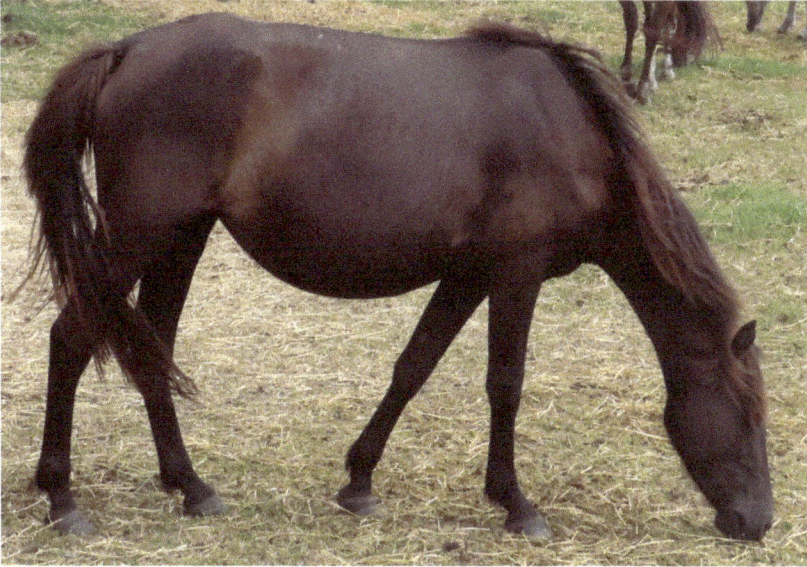

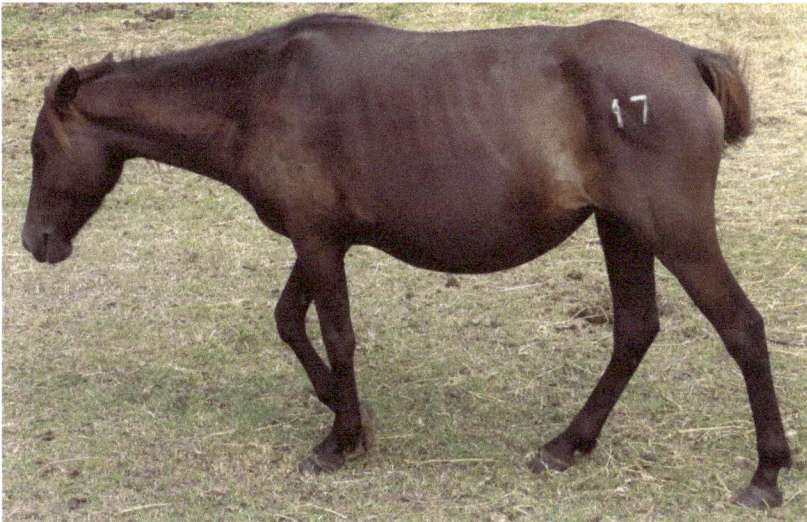

Black

Milly Sue

mare   birth year: 2017   brand: 17
SURFER'S RIPTIDE x LEAH'S BAYSIDE ANGEL

Brown eyes. Auction price: $9,000. First seen April 29, 2017.

Video Clip

Pedigree

Notes:

Milly Sue

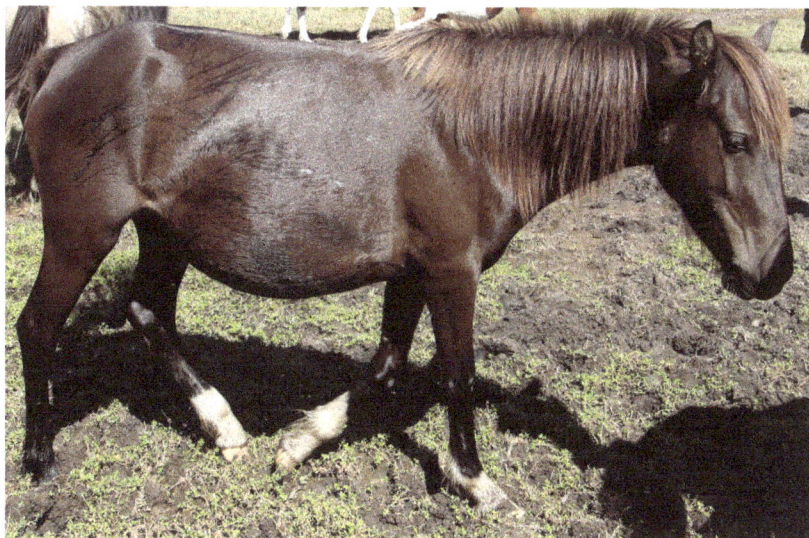

Black

CLG Surfer's Blue Moon

Blue, Blue Moon, Surfer's Blue Moon
mare   birth year: 2015   brand: 15
SURFER DUDE x GOT MILK

Blue eyes. Auction price: $25,000. Born April 27, 2015. Buyback donor: Chincoteague Legacy Group.

Video Clip   Pedigree

Notes:

CLG Surfer's Blue Moon

Black Comparison Chart

Name	Pg #	Brand	Mane	Face
Ace's Black Tie Affair	128	07	right	
CLG Ember	114	18	left	
CLG Surfer's Blue Moon	122	15	even	baldface
Dexter's Midnight Runner	116	19	right	
Milly Sue	120	17	right	
Talia/Evan's Angel	118	17	right	

NOTES

Ace's Black Tie Affair is included here even though he is technically a pinto. His markings are so minimal that he is routinely wrongly identified as solid black.

Left & right refers to the animal's left & right.

Mane: left = falls to the left **right** = falls to the right **split** = significant portion falls on left and right

Legs				Notable Details
R F	**R B**	**L F**	**L B**	
sock	stocking	sock	stocking	stallion; small upside heart behind left front leg
sock	sock	sock	sock	blue eyes
sock		sock	sock	7 in brand easily mistaken for 1

R F = right front   **R B** = right back   **L F** = left front   **L B** = left back
sock = white well below the knee   **stocking** = white near and above the knee

baldface = white covers most of the face   **blaze** = white streak running down the length of the face   **snip** = white spot on the muzzle   **star** = white spot on the forehead

Black Pinto

Ace's Miss Raven Rhapsody

Raven Rhapsody, Raven
mare   birth year: 2020   brand: 20
ACE'S BLACK TIE AFFAIR x MARINA'S MARSH MALLOW

Brown eyes. Auction price: $28,250. First seen June 19, 2020. Buyback donor: Audra, Alexandra, and Teresa Swain.

Video Clip

Pedigree

Notes:

Ace's Miss Raven Rhapsody

Black Pinto

Ace's Black Tie Affair

Ace
stallion   birth year: 2007   brand: 07
Centaur x Susie Q

Brown eyes. Auction price: $9,500. Born May 1, 2007. Buyback donor: Folsom family. Alternate sire: Charcoal/N9BNZ.

Video Clip

Pedigree

Notes:

Ace's Black Tie Affair

Black Pinto

Poco's Starry Night

Starry Night, Cash
mare   birth year: 2012   brand: 12
DON LEONARD STUD x POCO LATTE PW

Brown eyes. Auction price: $6,700. Born April 9, 2012. Buyback donator: Buyback Babes.

Video Clip   Pedigree

Notes:

Poco's Starry Night

Black Pinto

Shelley's Shell Search

Shelley

mare   birth year: 2021   brand: 21

ACE'S BLACK TIE AFFAIR x BLACK PEARL

Brown eyes. Auction price: $16,000. First seen May 21, 2021. Buyback donor: Cwen Cole.

Video Clip

Pedigree

Notes:

Shelley's Shell Search

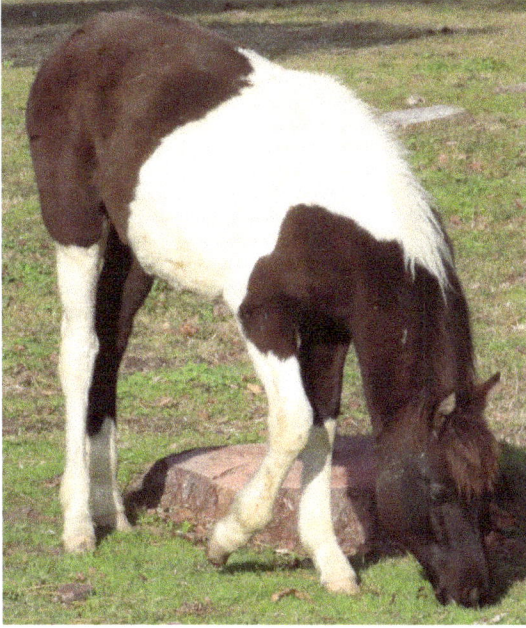

Black Pinto

Gracey

mare   birth year: 2013   brand: 13
SOCKETT TO ME x LEAH'S BAYSIDE ANGEL

Brown eyes. Auction price: $12,000. Born April 16, 2013. Buyback donator: Mark Zebley/ Janet Marabito.

Video Clip

Pedigree

Notes:

Gracey

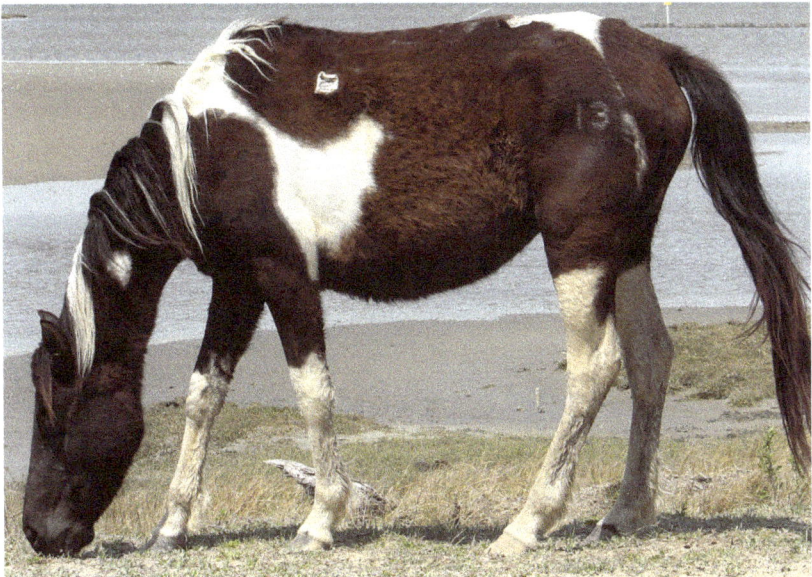

Black Pearl

Pearl
mare   birth year: 2014   brand: 14
SOCKETT TO ME x LEAH'S BAYSIDE ANGEL

Brown eyes. Auction price: $21,000. Buyback donor: Catherine Miller.

Video Clip

Pedigree

Notes:

Black Pearl

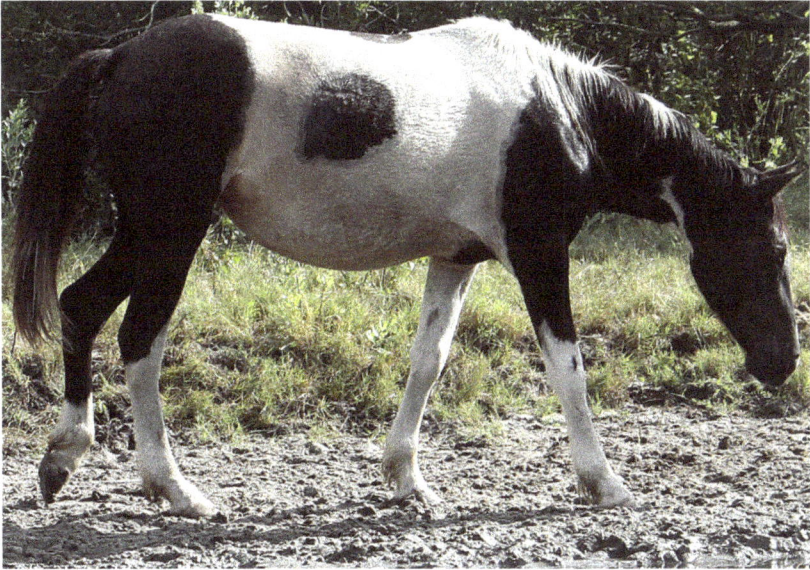

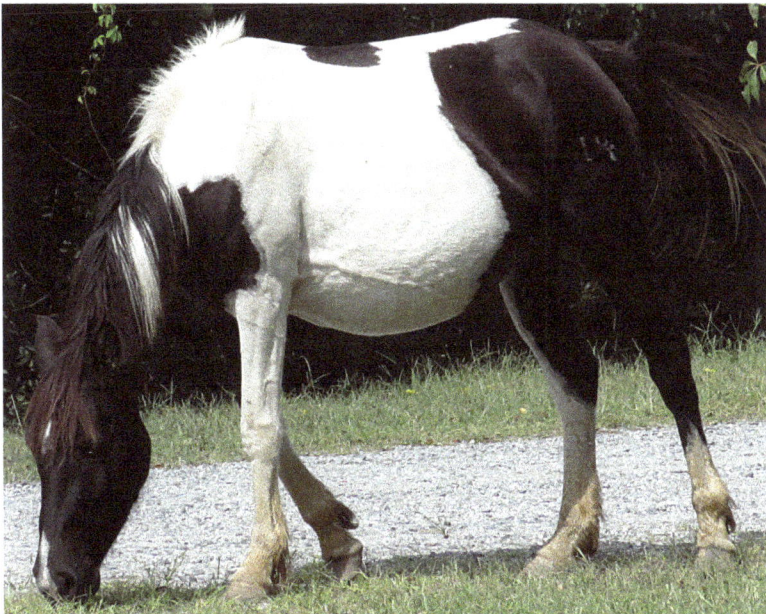

Baybe

Baby
mare   birth year: 2006   brand: none
TUFFER THAN LEATHER X APRIL MOON

Brown eyes. Donated to the CVFD in 2011 by the Leonard Family.

Video Clip

Pedigree

Notes:

Baybe

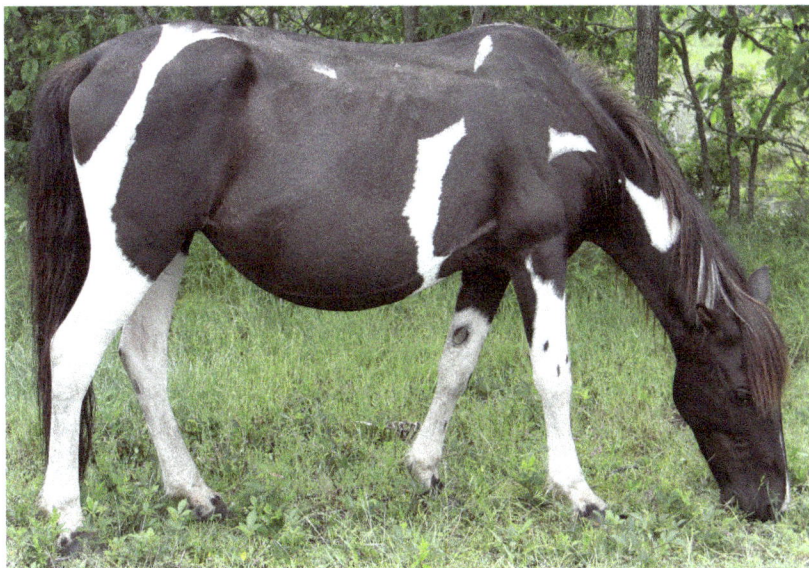

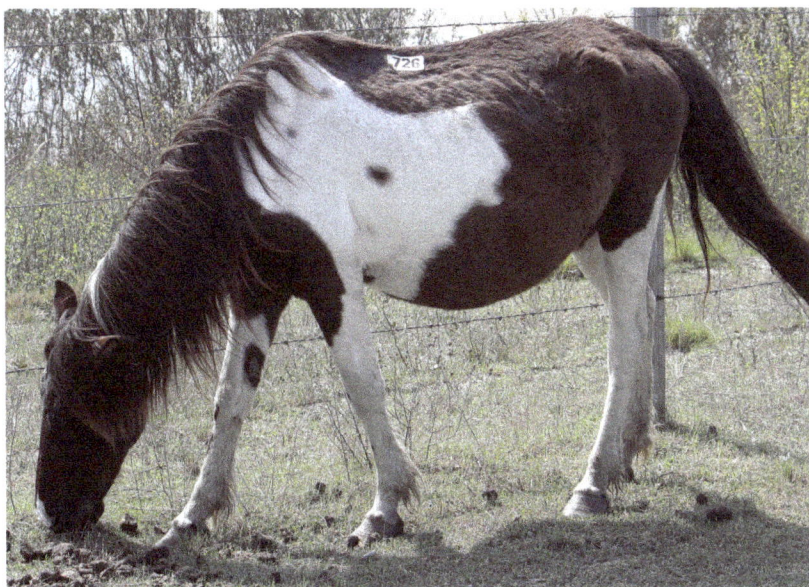

Black Pinto

CLG Magic Moment

Magic, Magic Moment
mare   birth year: 2020   brand: 20
Tornado's Legacy x A Splash of Freckles

Brown eyes. Auction price: $25,250. First seen May 31, 2020. Buyback donor: Chincoteague Legacy Group.

Video Clip

Pedigree

Notes:

CLG Magic Moment

Black Pinto

Beach Boy

Saltwater Renegade, Renegade
stallion   birth year: 2015   brand: 15
WH Nightwind x WH Sea Breeze

Brown eyes. Donated to the CVFC August 2015. Great Great Great Grandfoal of Misty.

Video Clip   Pedigree

Notes:

Beach Boy

Buckskin

Anne Bonny's Little Flower

Flower
mare   birth year: 2019   brand: 19
Tornado's Legacy x Anne Bonny

Brown eyes. Auction price: $12,500. First seen June 19, 2019. Buyback donor: Buy Back Babes.

Video Clip

Pedigree

Notes:

144

Anne Bonny's Little Flower

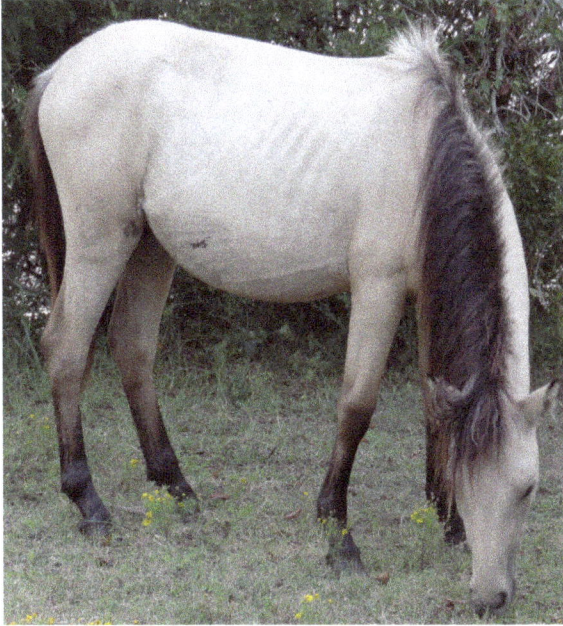

Buckskin

CLG Rider on the Storm

Rider, Storm
stallion   birth year: 2019   brand: 19
TORNADO'S LEGACY x MIRACLE'S NATURAL BEAUTY

Brown eyes. Auction price: $16,500. First seen April 15, 2019. Buyback donor: Chincoteague Legacy Group.

Video Clip   Pedigree

Notes:

CLG Rider on the Storm

Buckskin

Fancy Free

mare   birth year: 2021   brand: 21
EFFIE'S PAPA BEAR x LIZ'S SERENITY

Brown eyes. Auction price: $13,600. First seen July 8, 2021. Buyback donor: Cheryl Kornegay.

Video Clip

Pedigree

Notes:

Fancy Free

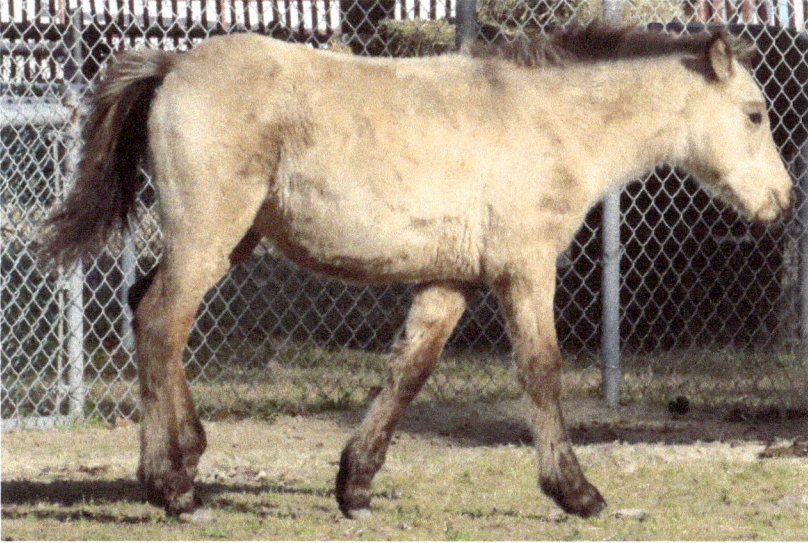

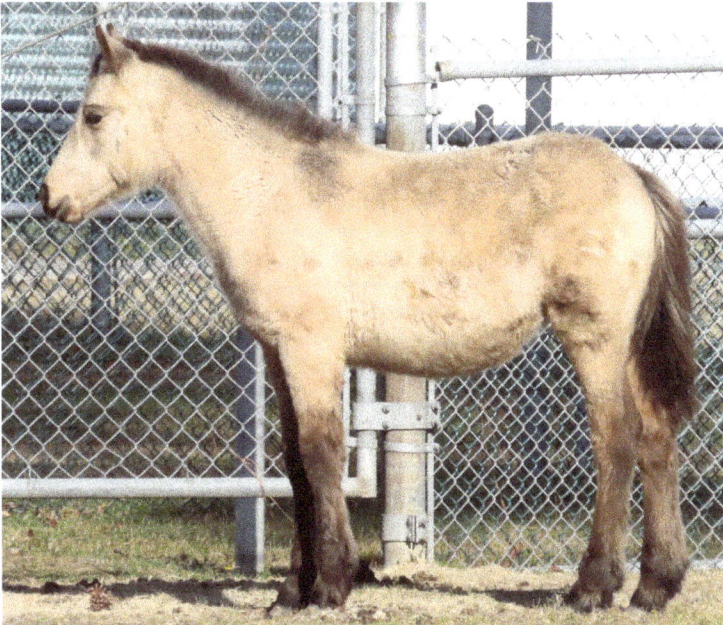

Buckskin

Ivana Marie Zustan

Zustan
mare   birth year: 2016   brand: 16
LITTLE DOLPHIN X JESSICA'S SEA STAR SANDY

Brown eye. Auction price: $5,700. Born May 19, 2016.

Notes:

Ivana Marie Zustan

Buckskin

Jessica's Sea Star Sandy

Jessica's Sandy
mare   birth year: 2006   brand: 06
TORNADO x PHILLY GIRL

Brown eyes. Auction price: $5,300. Born May 17, 2006. Buyback donor: Debbie Elliott-Fisk.

Video Clip

Pedigree

Notes:

Buckskin

Jessica's Sea Star Sandy

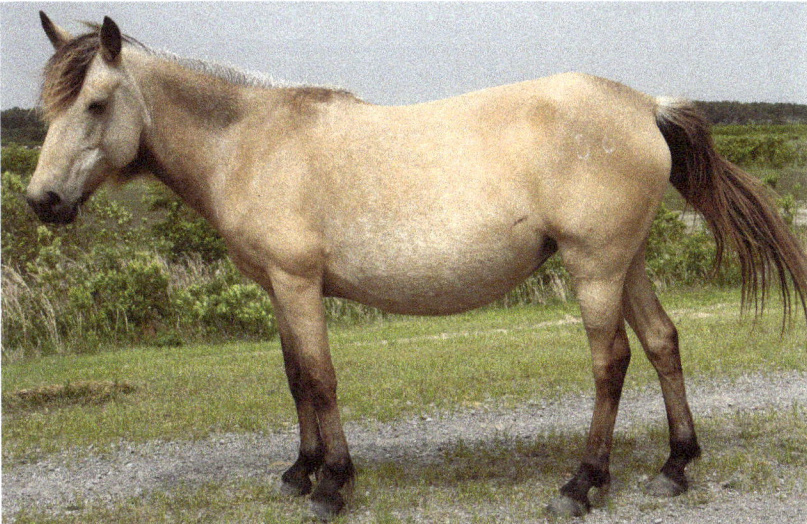

Buckskin

Liz's Serenity

Serenity
mare   birth year: 2017   brand: 17
WILD BILL x LANDRIE'S GEORGIA PEACH

Brown eyes. Auction price: $10,000. First seen April 26, 2017. Buyback donor: In memory of Liz Spino by family and friends.

Video Clip   Pedigree

Notes:

Liz's Serenity

Buckskin

Poco Latte PW

mare   birth year: 2002   brand: 02
Gunner's Moon x Misty Dawn

Brown eyes. Auction price: $6,750. Born July 15, 2002.

Video Clip   Pedigree

Notes:

Poco Latte PW

Buckskin

Sunrise Ocean Tides

Sunny
mare   birth year: 2015   brand: 15
LITTLE DOLPHIN x JESSICA'S SEA STAR SANDY

Brown eyes. Auction price: $3,100. Born May 29, 2015. Buyback donor: Lowrey Family.

Video Clip

Pedigree

Notes:

158

Sunrise Ocean Tides

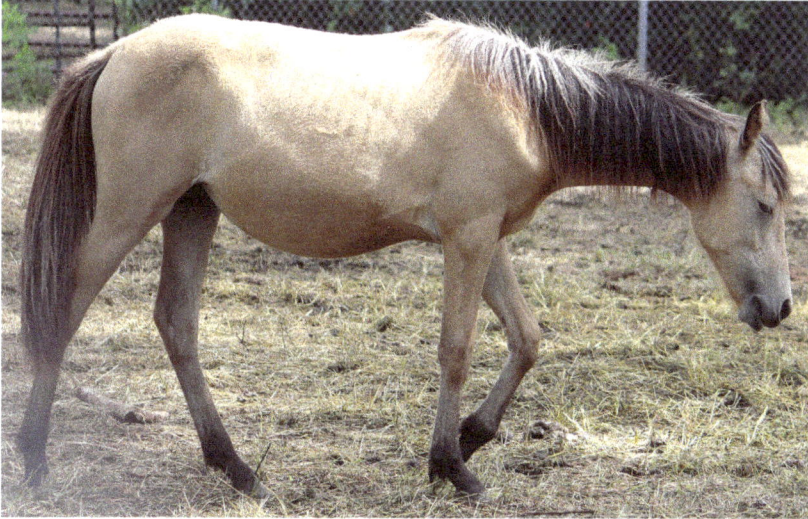

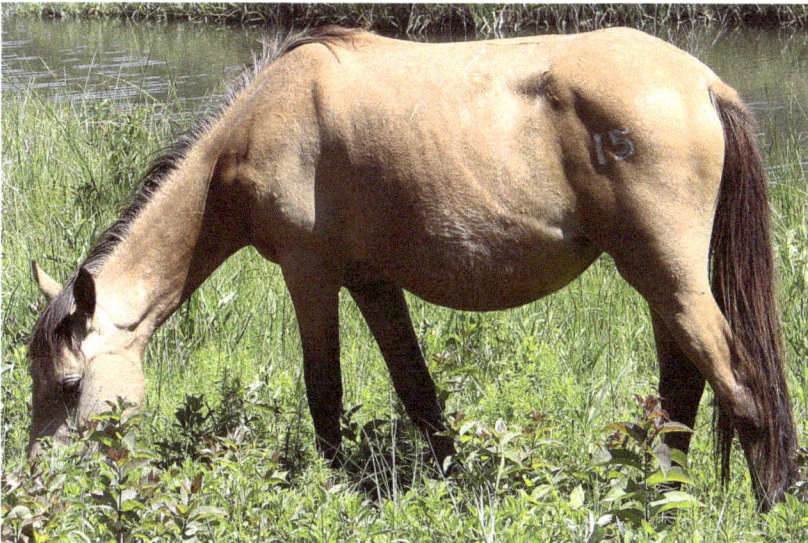

Buckskin

Kachina Grand Star

Kachina
mare   birth year: 2005   brand: 05, partial
NORTH STAR x TOO GRAND

Brown eyes. Auction price: $4,000. Born June 3, 2005. Buyback donor: Ginny Zelevitch and Joanne Rome.

Video Clip   Pedigree

Notes:

Kachina Grand Star

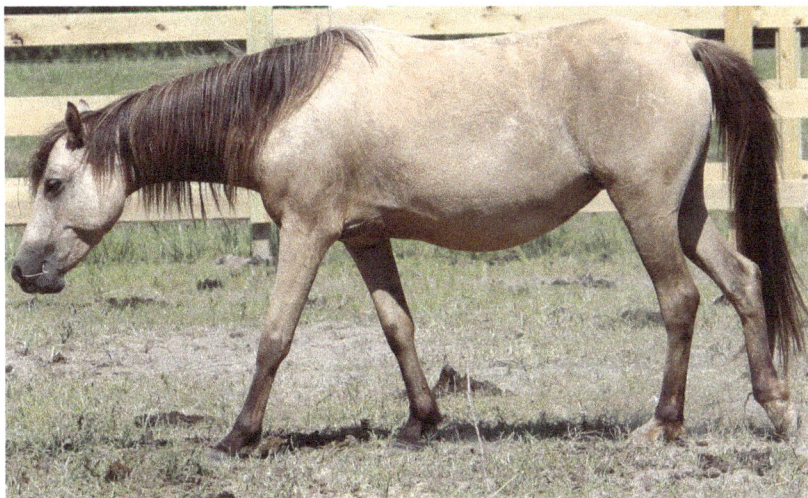

Buckskin Comparison Chart

Name	Pg #	Brand	Mane	Face
Anne Bonny's Little Flower	144	19	right	
CLG Rider on the Storm	146	19	right	
Fancy Free	148	21		
Ivana Marie Zustan	150	16	right	
Jessica's Sea Star Sandy	152	06	right	
Kachina Grand Star	160	05, partial	left	star
Liz's Serenity	154	17	right	
Poco Latte PW	156	02	right	
Sunrise Ocean Tides	158	15	right	

NOTES

Left & right refers to the animal's left & right.

Mane: left = falls to the left **right** = falls to the right **split** = significant portion falls on left and right

Legs				Notable Details
R F	R B	L F	L B	
				stallion
	sock		sock	
				dark dappled coat

R F = right front   **R B** = right back   **L F** = left front   **L B** = left back
sock = white well below the knee   **stocking** = white near and above the knee

baldface = white covers most of the face   **blaze** = white streak running down the length of the face   **snip** = white spot on the muzzle   **star** = white spot on the forehead

Buckskin Pinto

Molly's Rosebud

Rosie

mare   birth year: 2010   brand: none

Yankee Spirit x Merry Teapot's High Bid

Brown eyes. Auction price: $5,800. Born May 4, 2010.

Video Clip

Pedigree

Notes:

164

Molly's Rosebud

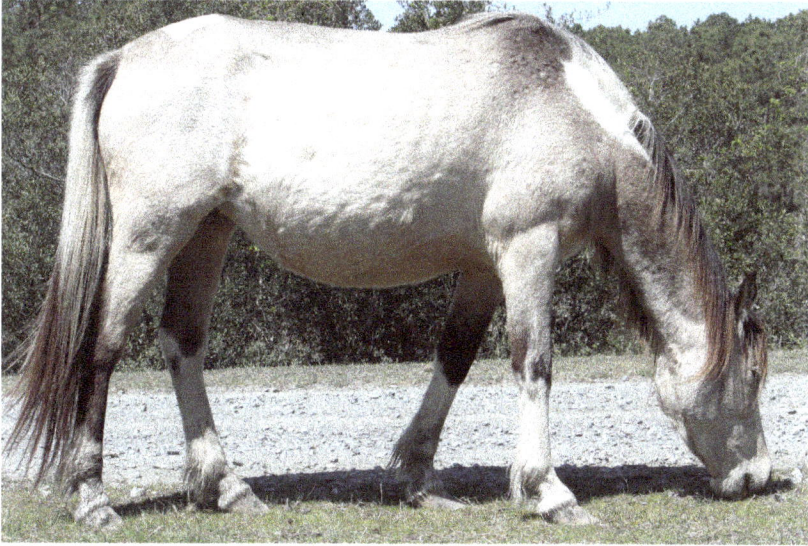

CLG Bay Princess

Bay Princess
mare   birth year: 2016   brand: 16
Tornado's Prince of Tides x Baybe

Brown eyes. Auction price: $10,000. First seen April 22, 2016. Buyback donor: Chincoteague Legacy Group.

Video Clip

Pedigree

Notes:

CLG Bay Princess

Buckskin Pinto

Loughlin's Luck of the Irish

Shamrock, Lucky
mare   birth year: 2021   brand: 21
TORNADO'S LEGACY x TIGER LILY

Brown eyes. Auction price: $12,000. Born June 28, 2021. Buyback donor: Fuccello Family.

Video Clip

Pedigree

Notes:

Loughlin's Luck of the Irish

Buckskin Pinto

CLG ToMorrow's Tidewater Twist

Twist, Triple T, Tidewater Twist
stallion   birth year: 2017   brand: 17
TORNADO'S LEGACY X SWEETHEART

Brown eyes. Auction price: $8,400. First seen March 13, 2017. Buyback donor: Chincoteague Legacy Group.

Video Clip   Pedigree

Notes:

CLG ToMorrow's Tidewater Twist

Buckskin Pinto

Badabing

mare   birth year: 2015   brand: 15

Tornado's Prince of Tides x Ella of Assateague

Brown eyes. Auction price: $4,500. Born May 12, 2015. Buyback donors: Julie Barry, Yuki Banks, and Linda Cook.

Video Clip   Pedigree

Notes:

Badabing

Buckskin Pinto

Tornado's Legacy

Legacy, Lil Tornado
stallion   birth year: 2007   brand: 07
TORNADO x UNCI

Brown eyes. Auction price: $11,000. Born April 3, 2007.

Video Clip   Pedigree

Notes:

Tornado's Legacy

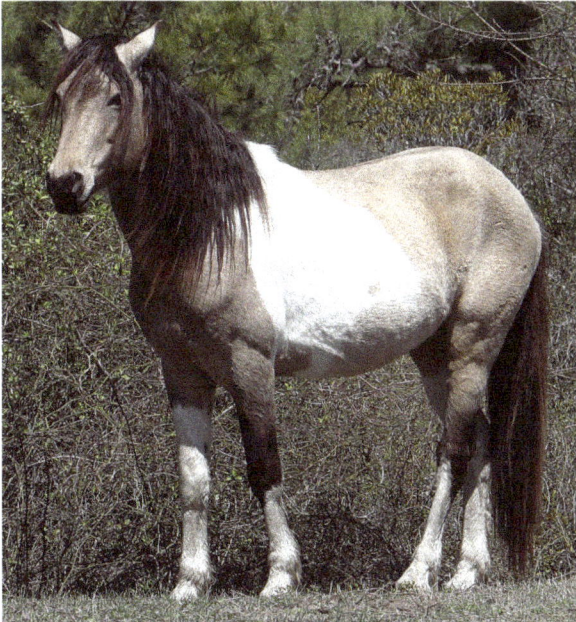

Buckskin Pinto

Ms Shampine

mare   birth year: 2021   brand: 21
(UNKNOWN) x MOLLY'S ROSEBUD

Brown eyes. Auction price: $13,100. First seen June 18, 2021. Buyback donor: Wanda and George Panos.

Video Clip

Pedigree

Notes:

Ms Shampine

Buckskin Pinto

Randy

mare   birth year: 2014   brand: 14
TORNADO'S PRINCE OF TIDES x BAYBE

Brown eyes. Auction price: $8,100. Buyback donator: Heckman Family.

Video Clip   Pedigree

Notes:

Randy

Buckskin Pinto

Serendipity

mare   birth year: 2018   brand: 18
MAVERICK x CALCETÍN

Brown eyes. Auction price: $8,200. Alternate sire: Ace's Black Tie Affair. First seen April 29, 2018. Buyback donor: Gina Marabito Zebley.

Video Clip   Pedigree

Notes:

Serendipity

Buckskin Pinto

Tidewater Treasure

Treasure
mare   birth year: 2000   brand: none
CHEROKEE CHIEF x BLONDE

Brown eyes. Donated to CVFC December 2018.

Video Clip

Pedigree

Notes:

Tidewater Treasure

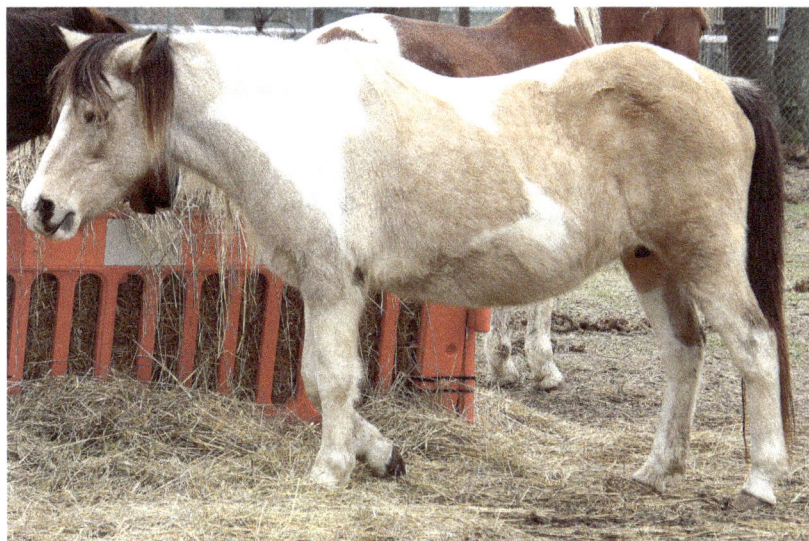

Chestnut

JABATAA

mare   birth year: 2002 brand: 02
CHEROKEE CHIEF x ROSIE O' GRADY

Brown eyes. Auction price: $4,900. Born July 2002. Buyback donor: Mauger family.

Video Clip   Pedigree

Notes:

Chestnut

JABATAA

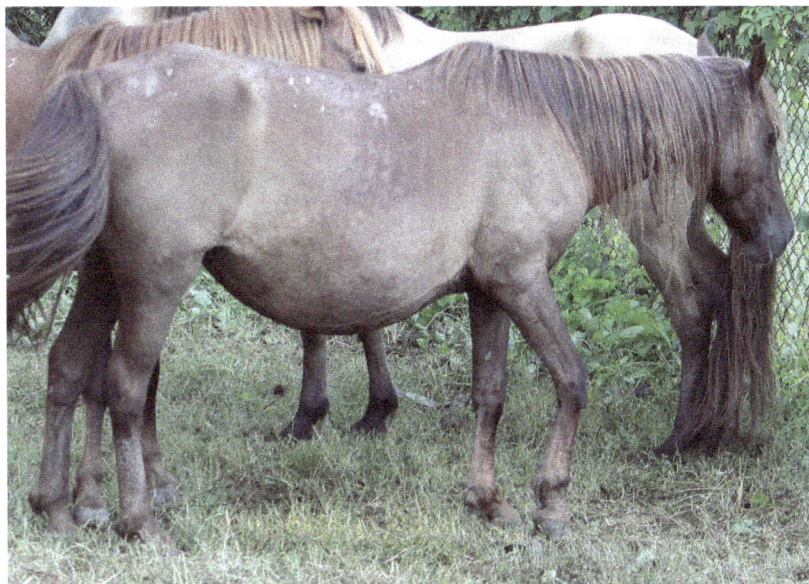

Chestnut

Surfer's Shining Star

Gingersnap
mare   birth year: 2015   brand: 15
SURFER DUDE x TSG's ELUSIVE STAR

Brown eyes. Auction price: $6,500. Born March 23, 2015. Buyback donor: Joyce Westberry.

Video Clip

Pedigree

Notes:

Surfer's Shining Star

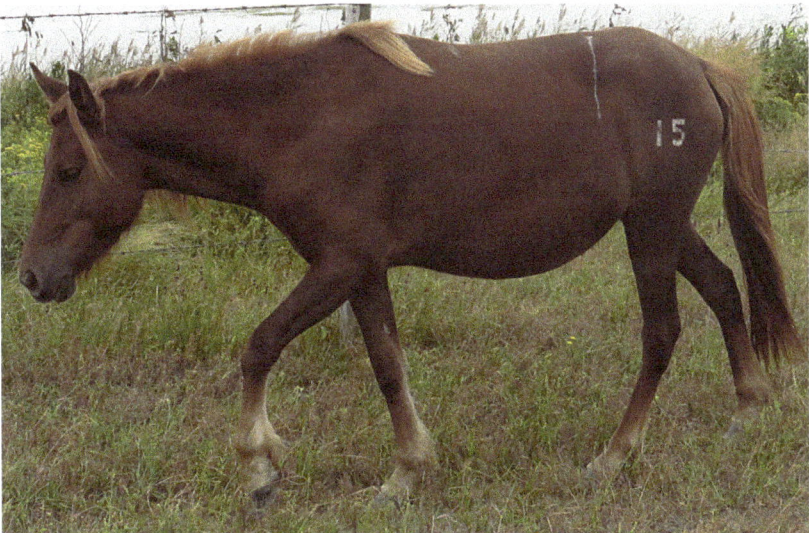

Chestnut

Surfin' Chantel

mare   birth year: 2013   brand: 13
RAINBOW WARRIOR x SURFIN' SCARLET

Brown eyes. Born September 2013. Fall buyback.

Video Clip

Pedigree

Notes:

Surfin' Chantel

Chestnut

Susana

mare   birth year: 2001   brand: 01
CHEROKEE CHIEF x GLAMOUR GIRL

Brown eyes. Born July 20, 2001. Buyback donor: Strothoff family.

Video Clip

Pedigree

Notes:

Susana

Chestnut

Suzy's Sweetheart

mare   birth year: 1998   brand: 98
CHEROKEE CHIEF X VOYAGER

Brown eyes. Born July 1998. Buyback donor: Trice family.

Video Clip

Pedigree

Notes:

Suzy's Sweetheart

Chestnut

Sue's Crown of Hope

Hope
mare   birth year: 2019   brand: 19
KEN x KIMMEE-SUE

Brown eyes. Auction price: $1,600. First seen May 14, 2019. Buyback donor: Joe Lowery, In memory of Sue Wingfield Lowery by family and friends.

Video Clip

Pedigree

Notes:

Sue's Crown of Hope

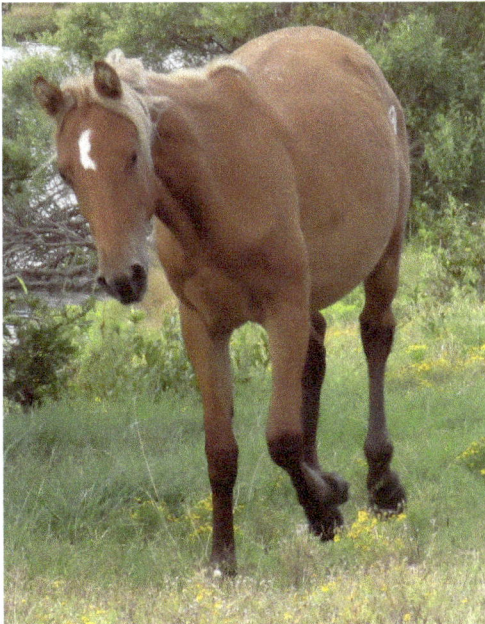

Chestnut

Surfin' Scarlet

Scarlet
mare   birth year: 2000   brand: 00
SURFER DUDE x SURF QUEEN

Brown eyes. Born July 2000. Buyback donor: Strand family.

Video Clip **Pedigree**

Notes:

Surfin' Scarlet

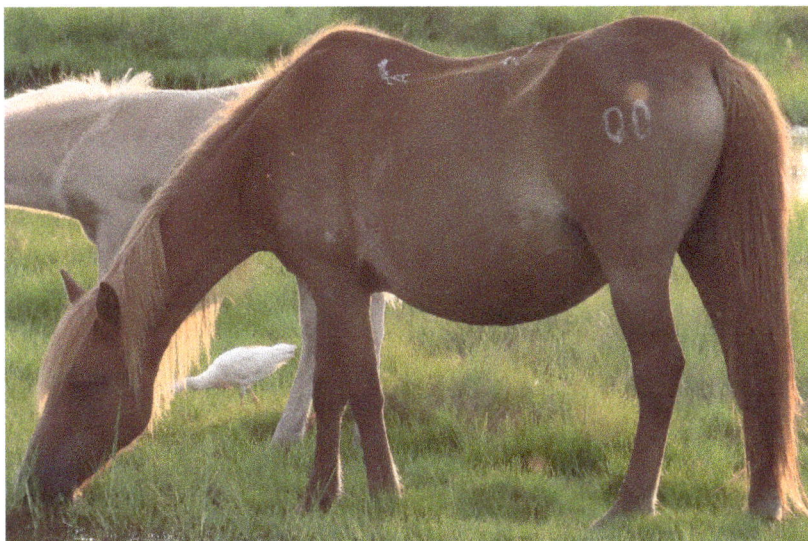

Chestnut

Tuleta Star

mare   birth year: 2002   brand: 02
CHEROKEE CHIEF x A TOUCH OF DUST

Brown eyes. Auction price: $5,000. Born July 17, 2002. Buyback donor: Tuleta White.

Video Clip

Pedigree

Notes:

Tuleta Star

Chestnut

Kimmee-Sue

mare   birth year: 2012   brand: 12
Courtney's Boy x Cinnamon Blaze

Brown eyes. Auction price: $5,000. Born May 2, 2012. Buyback donator: Sue Fitzgerald.

Video Clip   Pedigree

Notes:

Kimmee-Sue

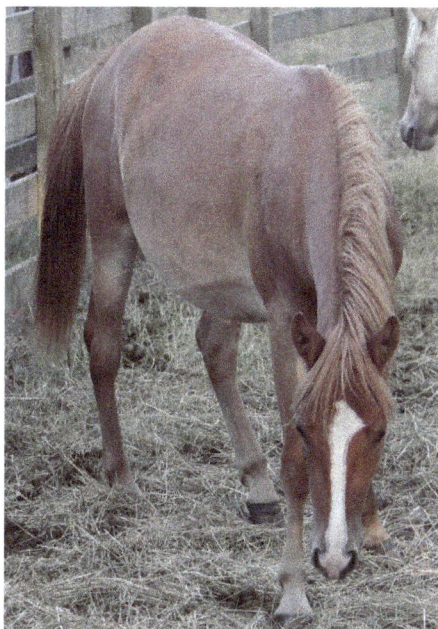

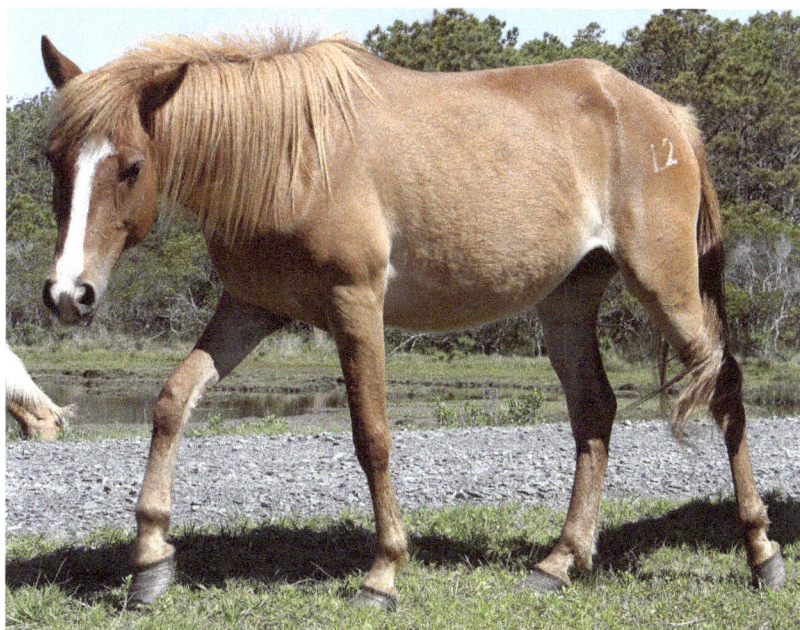

Chestnut

Precious Jewel

mare   birth year: 2014   brand: 14
PHANTOM MIST x UNCI

Brown eyes. Auction price: $5,200. Buyback donator: Sibyl and Elton Wright.

Notes:

_____

_____

_____

_____

_____

_____

_____

_____

Precious Jewel

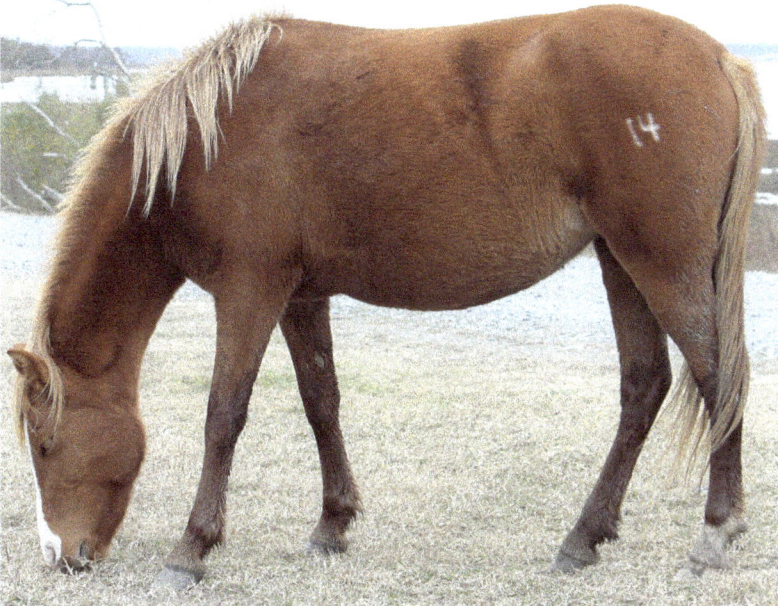

Chestnut

CLG Pennies From Heaven

Penny
mare   birth year: 2021   brand: 21
WILD THING x TULETA STAR

Brown eyes. Auction price: $25,500. First seen April 11, 2021. Buyback donor: Chincoteague Legacy Group.

Notes:

CLG Pennies From Heaven

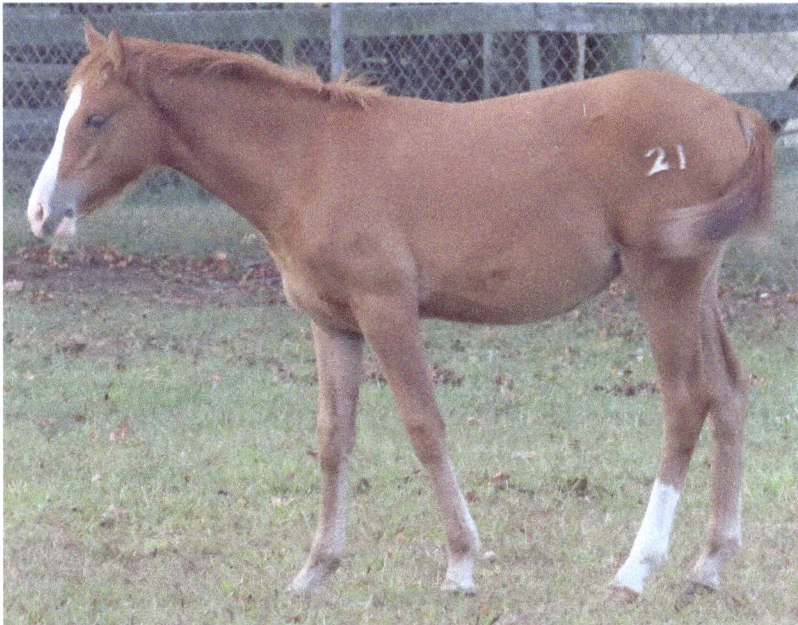

Chestnut

Judy's Little Smooch

Smooch
mare   birth year: 2016   brand: none
SURFER'S RIPTIDE x BUTTERFLY KISSES

Brown eyes. Born August 9, 2016. Buyback donor: Judy Fuccello.

Video Clip

Pedigree

Notes:

Judy's Little Smooch

Chestnut

Moonbeam

N2BHS-CKPT
mare   birth year: 2021   brand: 21, F
Joy x Moonshadow

Brown eyes. Born April 5, 2021. Transferred to CVFC July 12, 2021.

Deemed too delicate to live on Assateague. Moved to private farm.

Notes:

Moonbeam

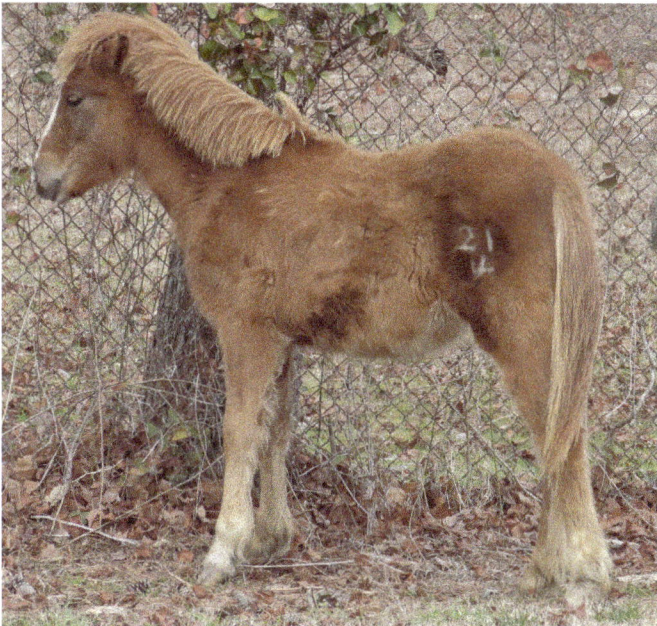

Chestnut

Surfer Dude's Gidget

Gidget
mare   birth year: 2002   brand: F, 02, partial

Surfer Dude x Virginia Belle

Brown eyes. Auction price: $7,800. Born March 12, 2002. Buyback donor: Buyback Babes.

Video Clip

Pedigree

Notes:

Surfer Dude's Gidget

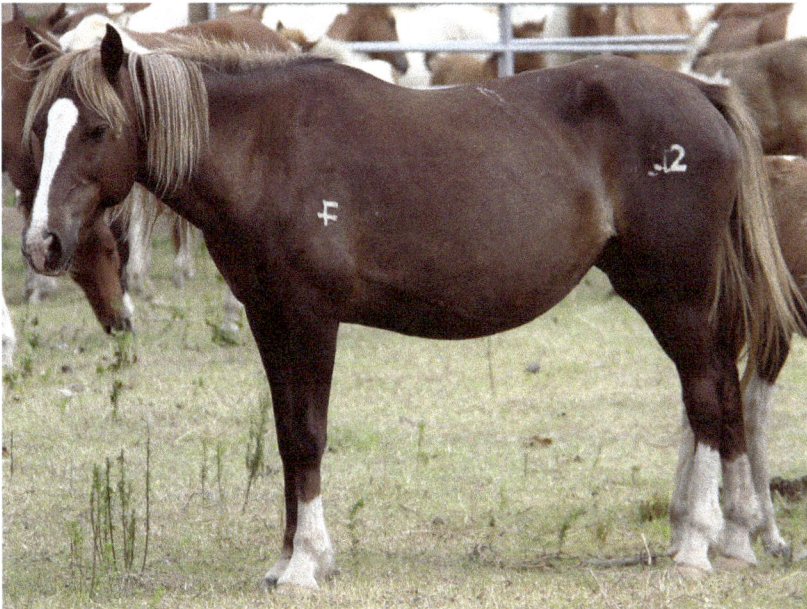

Chestnut

Dreamer's Gift

mare   birth year: 2012   brand: 12
SURFER DUDE x LYRA'S VEGA

Brown eyes. Auction price: $4,300. Buyback donor: Janey, Anna, and Amanda Beer. Alternate sire: Surfer's Riptide.

Video Clip

Pedigree

Notes:

Dreamer's Gift

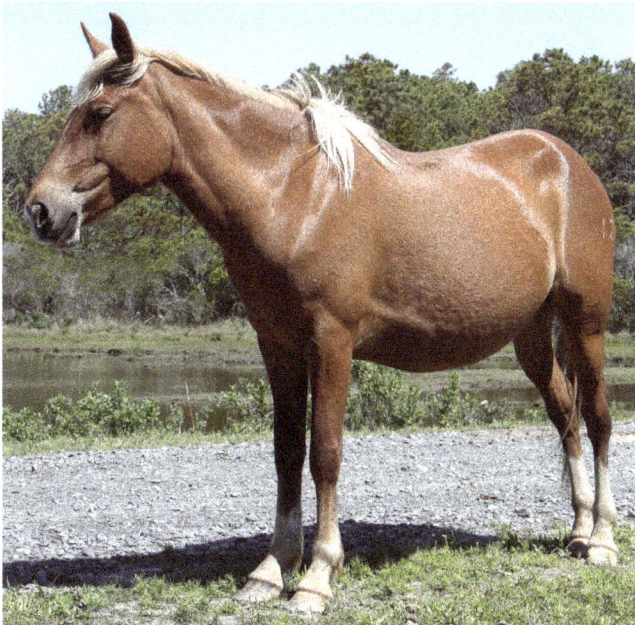

Chestnut

Surfer Princess

mare   birth year: 2015   brand: 15
Surfer Dude x Surf Queen

Brown eyes. Auction price: $5,300. Born May 14, 2015. Buyback donators: Julie Barry, Yuki Banks, and Linda Cook.

Video Clip

Pedigree

Notes:

Surfer Princess

Chestnut

Surfette

mare   birth year: 2017   brand: 17
WH Salt Marsh x Sundance

Brown eyes. Donated to CVFC March 2018. Great Great Great Great Grandfoal of Misty.

Video Clip

Pedigree

Notes:

Surfette

Chestnut

Ken

Valentine
stallion   birth year: 2008   brand: 08
WILD THING x STAR GAZER

Brown eyes. Auction price: $4,500. Born February 14, 2008. Alternate sire: Glacier. Buyback donator: Sue Lowery.

Video Clip

Pedigree

Notes:

Ken

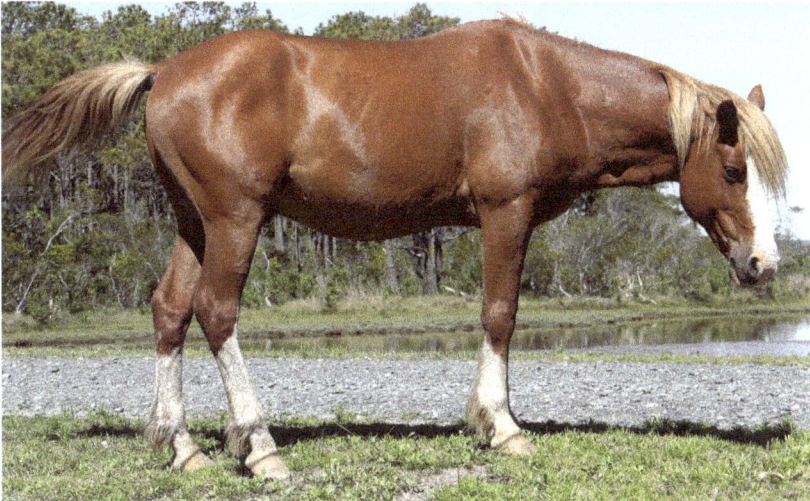

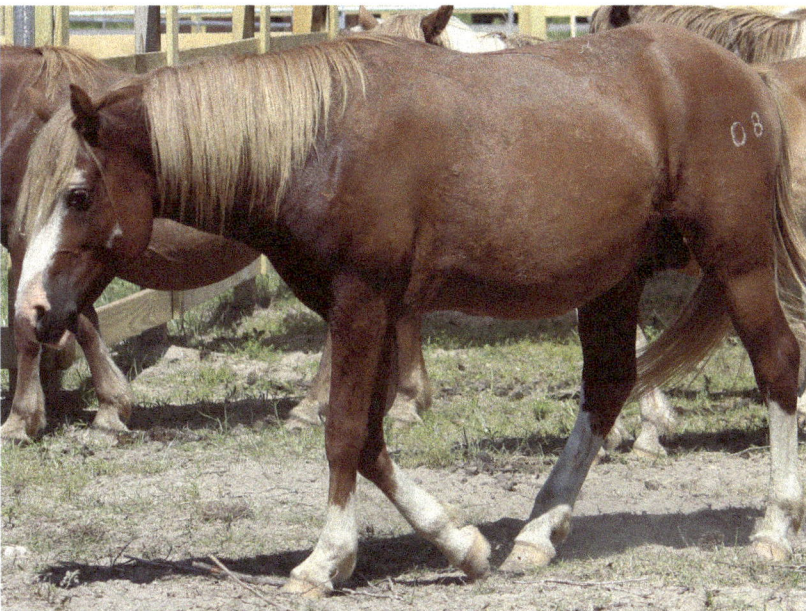

Chestnut

Dreamer's Stardust

Stardust
mare   birth year: 2018   brand: 18
KEN x DREAMER'S GIFT

Brown eyes. First seen March 8, 2018. Buyback donor: Beer Family.

Video Clip   Pedigree

Notes:

Dreamer's Stardust

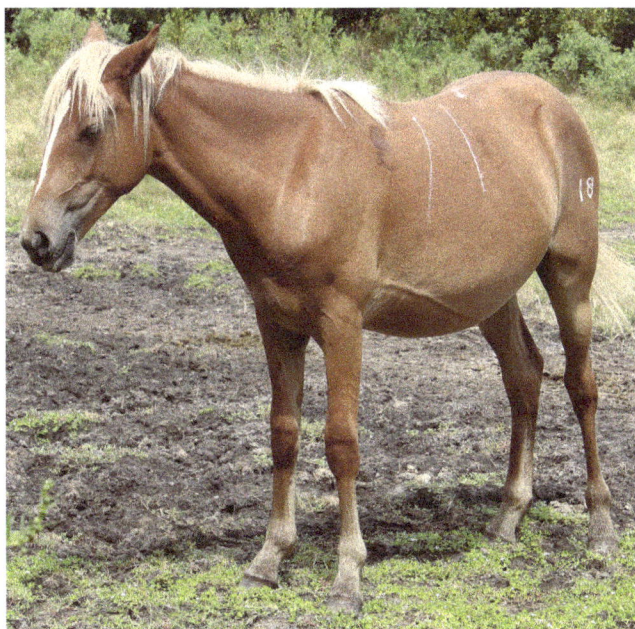

Chestnut

Surfer's Riptide

Riptide, Rip Tide
stallion   birth year: 2009   brand: 09, partial
SURFER DUDE X SURF QUEEN

Brown eyes. Auction price: $11,500. Born May 3, 2009. Buyback donor: Folsom family.

Video Clip

Pedigree

Notes:

Surfer's Riptide

Chestnut Comparison Chart

Name	Pg #	Brand	Mane	Face
CLG Pennies From Heaven	204	21	right	blaze
Dreamer's Gift	212	12	split	star and snip
Dreamer's Stardust	220	18	split	blaze
JABATAA	184	02	right	
Judy's Little Smooch	206		right	blaze
Ken	218	08	left	baldface
Kimmee-Sue	200	12	left	blaze
Moonbeam	208	21, F	left	blaze
Precious Jewel	202	14	split	blaze
Sue's Crown of Hope	194	19	right	star
Surfer Dude's Gidget	210	F, 02, partial	split	blaze
Surfer Princess	214	15	right	star and snip
Surfer's Riptide	222	09, partial	right	baldface
Surfer's Shining Star	186	15	right	
Surfette	216	17	right	blaze
Surfin' Chantel	188	13	right	
Surfin' Scarlet	196	00	right	star
Susana	190	01	right	
Suzy's Sweetheart	192	98	right	
Tuleta Star	198	02	right	star and snip

NOTES

Left & right refers to the animal's left & right.

Mane: left = falls to the left **right** = falls to the right **split** = significant portion falls on left and right

R F = right front **R B** = right back **L F** = left front **L B** = left back
sock = white well below the knee **stocking** = white near and above the knee

Legs				Notable Details
R F	R B	L F	L B	
			stocking	
sock	sock	sock	sock	blond mane & tail
stocking	stocking	stocking	stocking	blond mane & tail
				very dark coat
	stocking			
sock	stocking	sock	stocking	stallion; small white kiss mark on left cheek; blond mane & tail
		sock	sock	
			sock	
				large crescent shaped star; 1 in brand is smeared
	sock	sock	sock	dark coat; much lighter mane & tail
sock	sock	sock	sock	arrowhead shaped spot on left side
stocking	stocking	stocking	stocking	stallion; dark coat; blond mane & tail; long forelock covers eyes
				dark red coat; mane & tail a little lighter
sock	sock	sock	sock	dark brown
				small whitish diamond-shaped patch on right hip
				small stature
				long forelock

baldface = white covers most of the face   **blaze** = white streak running down the length of the face   **snip** = white spot on the muzzle   **star** = white spot on the forehead

Chestnut Pinto

Catwalk's Olympic Glory

Glory
mare   birth year: 2016   brand: 16
AJAX x CATWALK CHAOS

Brown eyes. Auction price: $8,100. Born May 2, 2016. Buyback donor: Leslie Joliet.

Video Clip

Pedigree

Notes:

Catwalk's Olympic Glory

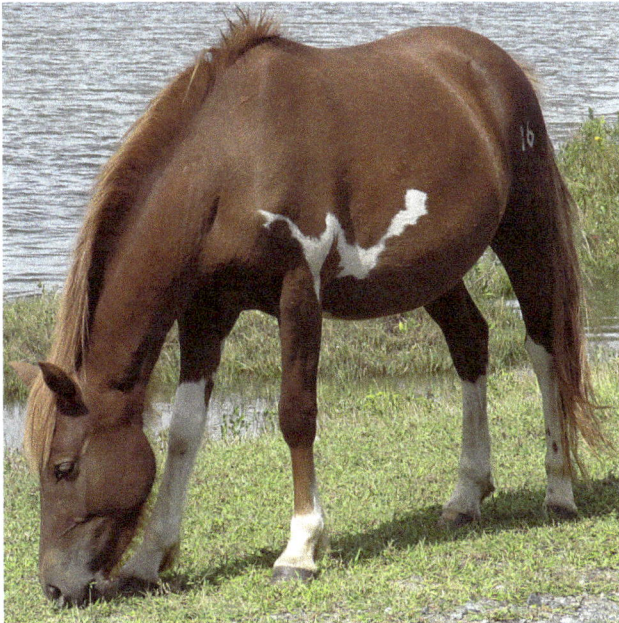

Chestnut Pinto

Chili

Lil Miss Hot Stuff
mare   birth year: 2016   brand: 17, partial
CHIEF GOLDEN EAGLE X CLOUDBURST

Brown eyes. Born September 24, 2016. Donated to CVFC March 2018.

Video Clip

Pedigree

Notes:

Chili

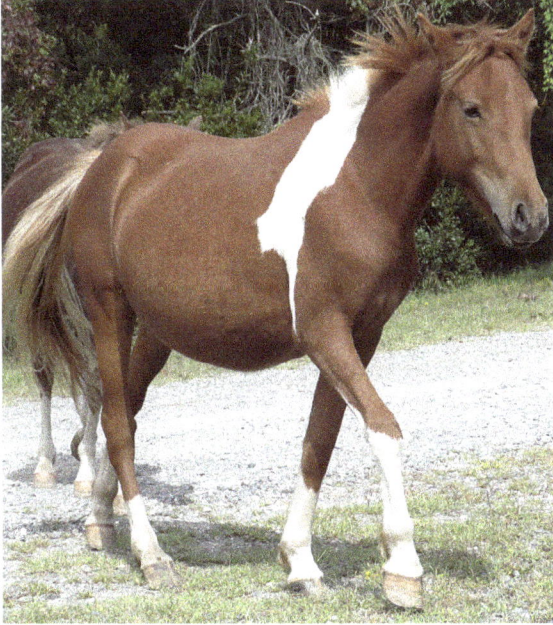

Chestnut Pinto

CJ SAMM'N

mare   birth year: 2006   brand: 06
NORTH STAR x SLASH OF WHITE

Brown eyes. Auction price: $3,700. Born May 7, 2006. Alternate sire: Leonard Stud.

Video Clip

Pedigree

Notes:

CJ SAMM'N

Chestnut Pinto

Kimball's Rainbow Delight

Rainy, Rainbow Delight
mare   birth year: 2006   brand: 06, partial
NORTH STAR x RAMBLING RUBY

Brown eyes. Auction price: $3,100. Born May 9, 2006. Buyback donator: Mary and Normal Kimball.

Notes:

Kimball's Rainbow Delight

Chestnut Pinto

Corrie's Little Miss Magic

Corrie
mare   birth year: 2021   brand: 21
Archer's Gambit x Scotty ET

Brown eyes. Auction price: $16,000. First seen April 12, 2021.

Video Clip

Pedigree

Notes:

Corrie's Little Miss Magic

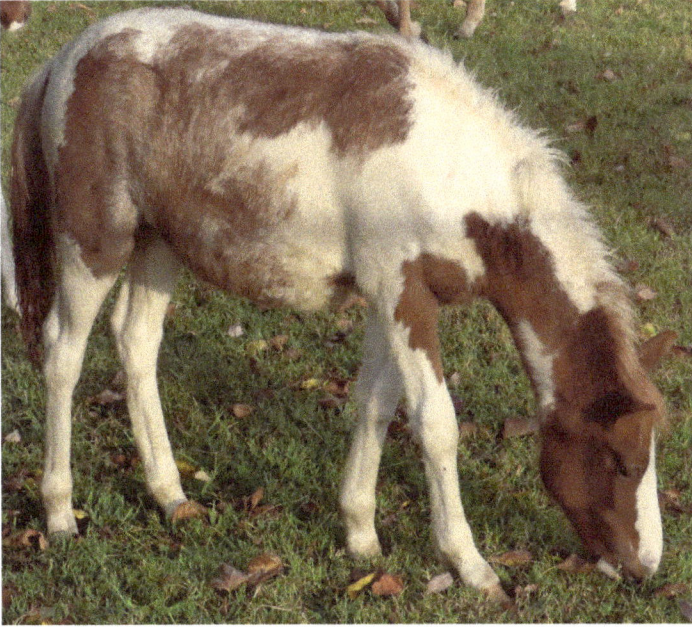

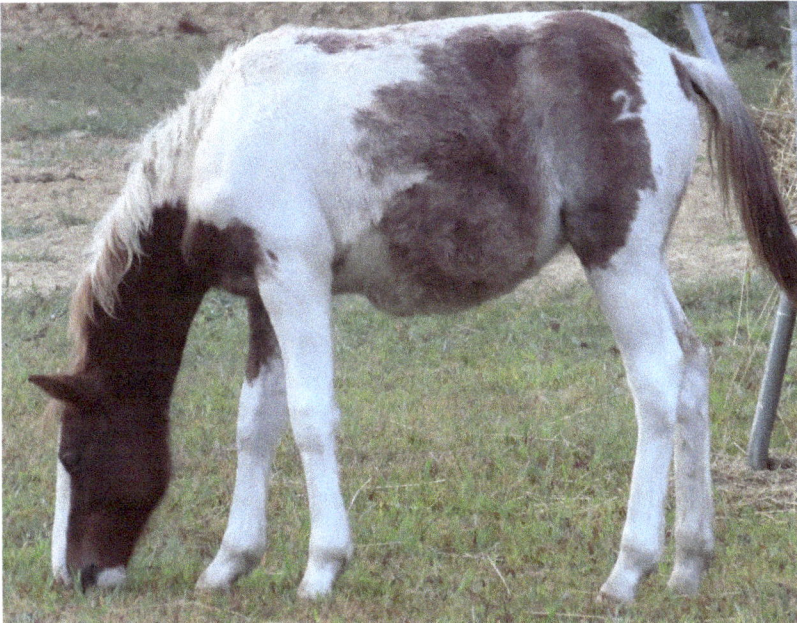

Chestnut Pinto

Tiger Lily

Waterbaby
mare   birth year: 2002   brand: none
CHEROKEE CHIEF x VOYAGER

Brown eyes. Born September 2002.

Notes:

Tiger Lily

Chestnut Pinto

Pony Girl's Bliss

Bliss
mare   birth year: 2017   brand: 17
Effie's Papa Bear x Carol's Little Freedom

Brown eyes. Auction price: $7,100. First seen June 4, 2017. Buyback donor: Cassou family.

Video Clip   Pedigree

Notes:

Pony Girl's Bliss

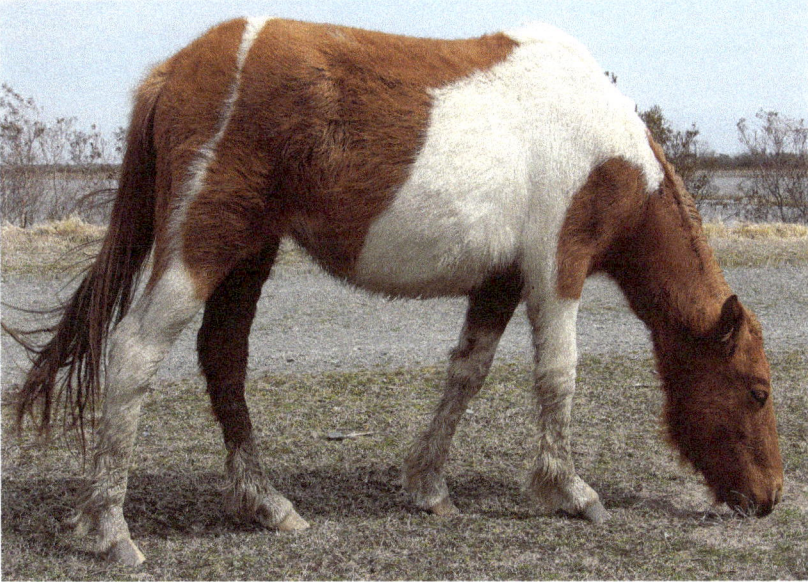

Chestnut Pinto

Catwalk Chaos

Margarita
mare   birth year: 2010   brand: none
CHAOS X PAINT BY NUMBER

Brown eyes. Auction price: $8,100. Born May 8, 2010.

Video Clip

Pedigree

Notes:

Catwalk Chaos

Chestnut Pinto

Carli Marie

mare   birth year: 2018   brand: 18
Ace's Black Tie Affair x Gidget's Beach Baby

Brown eyes. Auction price: $7,000. First seen April 29, 2018.

Video Clip

Pedigree

Notes:

Carli Marie

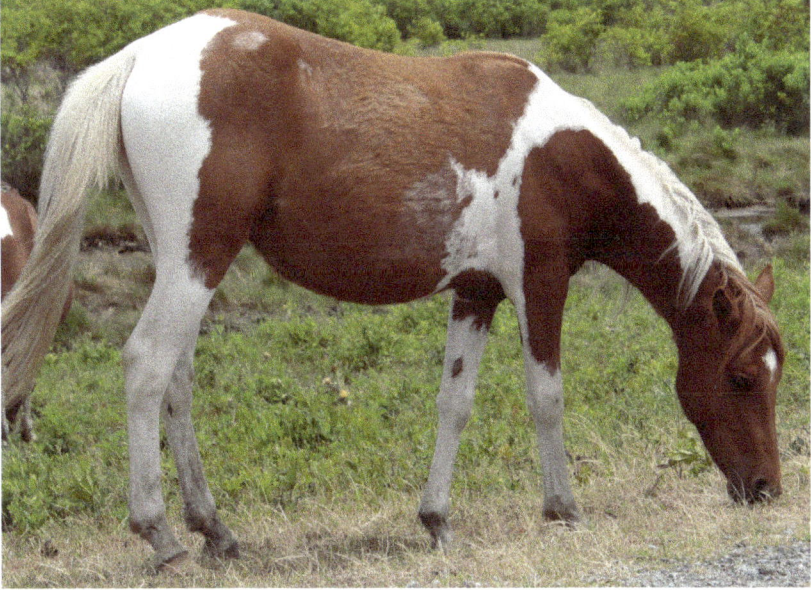

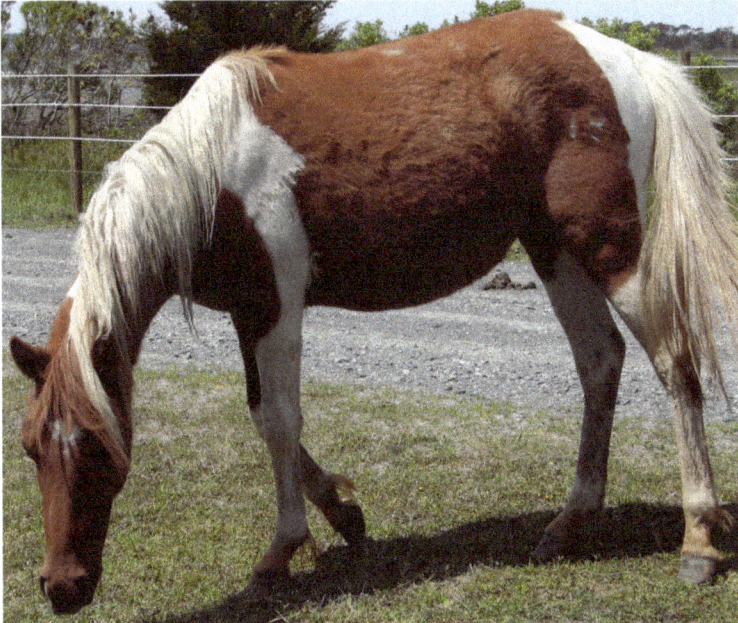

Chestnut Pinto

Anne Bonny

mare   birth year: 2011   brand: none
YANKEE SPIRIT x MYSTERY

Brown eyes. Auction price: $4,200. Born April 25, 2011. Buyback donor: Sarah Sickles.

Video Clip

Pedigree

Notes:

Anne Bonny

Chestnut Pinto

Sweet Jane

Duckie
mare   birth year: 2006   brand: 06, partial
COURTNEY'S BOY x LEFTY'S CHECKMARK

Brown eyes. Auction price: $4,200. Born April 6, 2006. Buyback donor: Sara Rasmussen.

Video Clip   Pedigree

Notes:

Sweet Jane

Chestnut Pinto

Little Duckie

Quackers
mare   birth year: 2011   brand: F
NORTH STAR x SWEET JANE

Brown eyes. Auction price: $3,200. Born May 28, 2011.

Video Clip

Pedigree

Notes:

Little Duckie

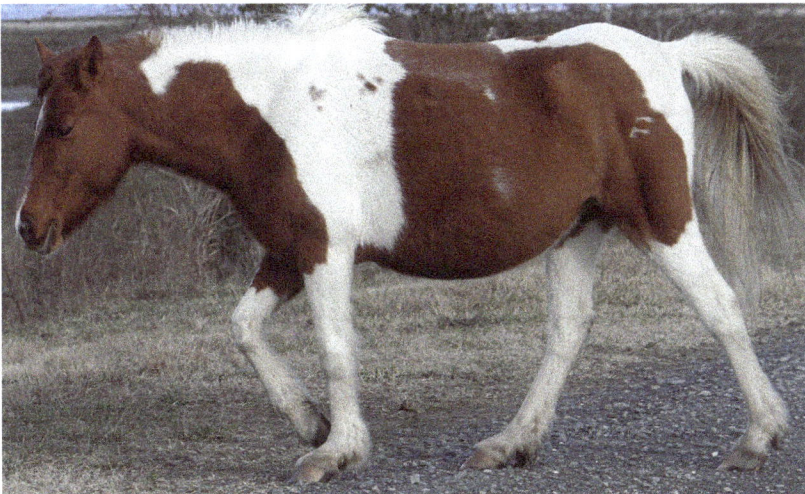

Chestnut Pinto

Two Teagues Taco's Chilibean

Chilibean
mare   birth year: 2019   brand: 19
ACE'S BLACK TIE AFFAIR x TWO TEAGUES TACO

Brown eyes. Auction price: $10,500. First seen June 19, 2019. Buyback donor: Buy Back Babes.

Notes:

Two Teagues Taco's Chilibean

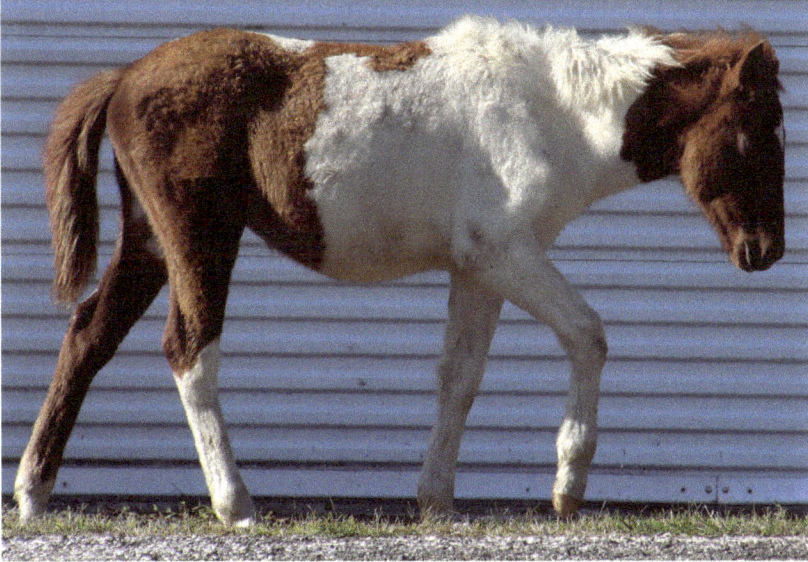

Chestnut Pinto

Misty Mills

mare   birth year: 2006   brand: 06, partial

COURTNEY'S BOY x SWEET MISCHIEF

Brown eyes. Auction price: $5,000. Born June 20, 2006.

Video Clip   Pedigree

Notes:

Misty Mills

Chestnut Pinto

Beach Bunny

mare   birth year: 2015   brand: 15
ARCHER'S GAMBIT X SWEET JANE

Brown eyes. Auction price: $6,000. Born May 13, 2015.

Video Clip

Pedigree

Notes:

Beach Bunny

Chestnut Pinto

Archer's Gambit

Puzzle, Little Frog
stallion   birth year: 2008   brand: 08
NORTH STAR x LILY PAD

Brown eyes. Auction price: $5,300. Born April 24, 2008.

Notes:

Archer's Gambit

Chestnut Pinto

Stevenson's Dakota Sky

Dakota, Dakota Sky
mare   birth year: 2001   brand: 01
COURTNEY'S BOY X PROMISE OF SUMMER

Brown eyes. Born July 17, 2001. Buyback donor: Catherine Young.

Video Clip

Pedigree

Notes:

Chestnut Pinto

Stevenson's Dakota Sky

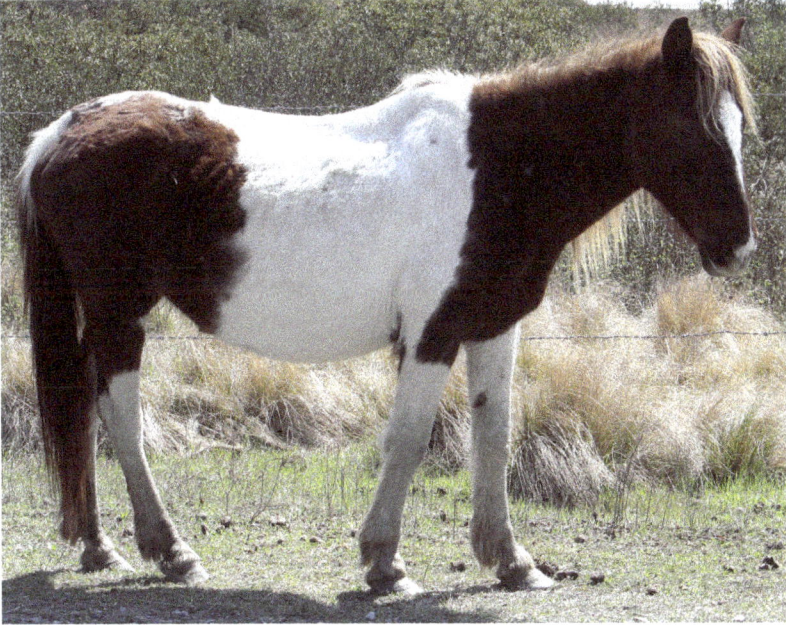

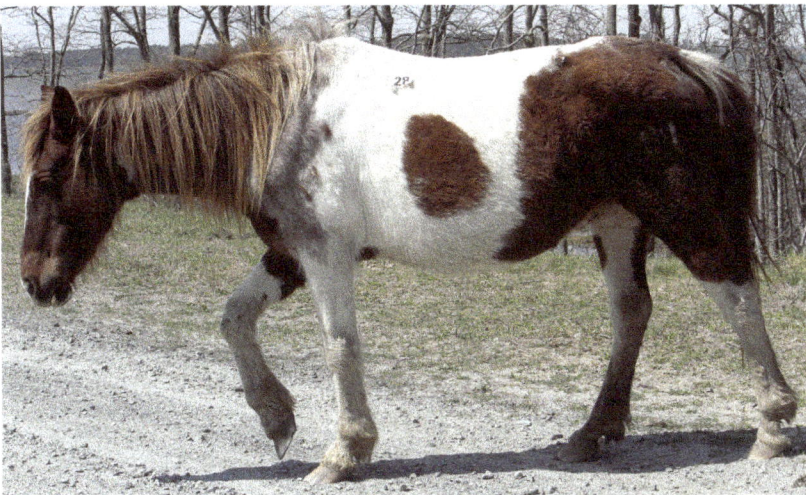

Chestnut Pinto

Myrt & Brenda's Indiana Girl

Indy, Indiana Girl
mare   birth year: 2020   brand: 20
MAVERICK X FIFTEEN FRIENDS OF FRECKLES

Brown eyes. Auction price: $18,250. First seen April 23, 2020. Buyback donor: Easton family.

Video Clip

Pedigree

Notes:

Myrt & Brenda's Indiana Girl

Chestnut Pinto

Sunny Skies After The Storm

Sunny Skies
mare   birth year: 2019   brand: 19
Archer's Gambit x Thunderstorm Skies

One blue, one brown eye. Auction price: $7,500. First seen April 27, 2019. Buyback donor: Mary and Claire Stiehm.

Video Clip

Pedigree

Notes:

Chestnut Pinto

Sunny Skies After The Storm

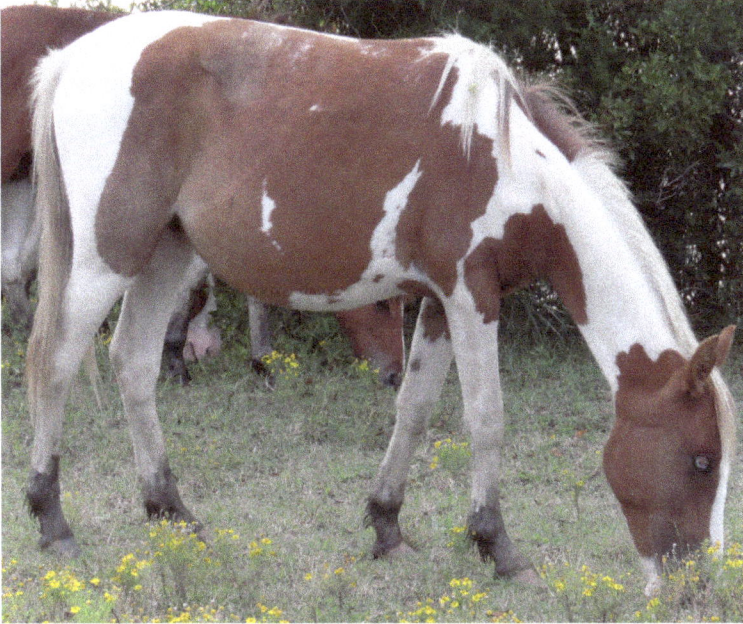

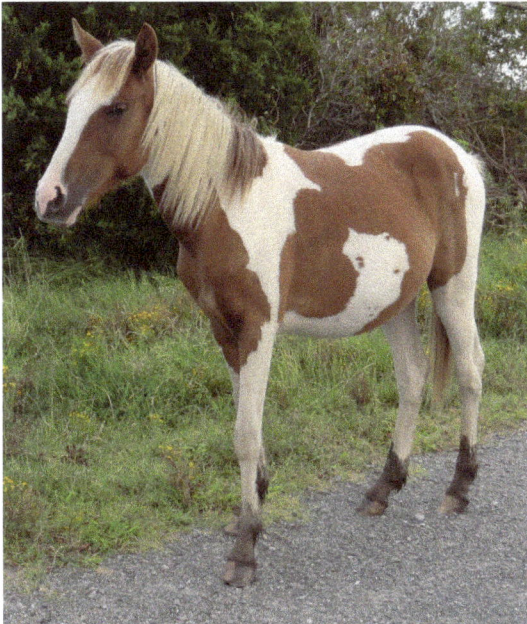

Chestnut Pinto

Clara's Glory

Clara
mare   birth year: 2020   brand: 20
TORNADO'S LEGACY x CATWALK'S OLYMPIC GLORY

Brown eyes. Auction price: $15,500. First seen June 18, 2020.

Video Clip

Pedigree

Notes:

Clara's Glory

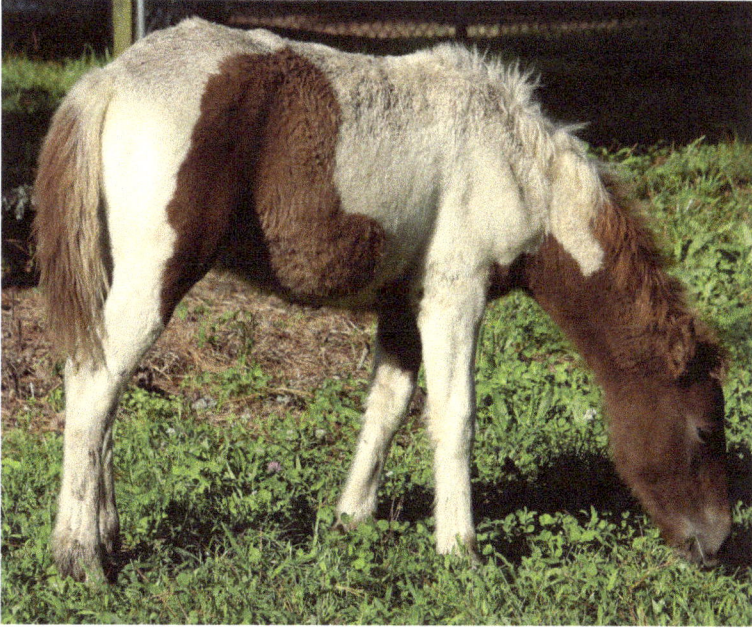

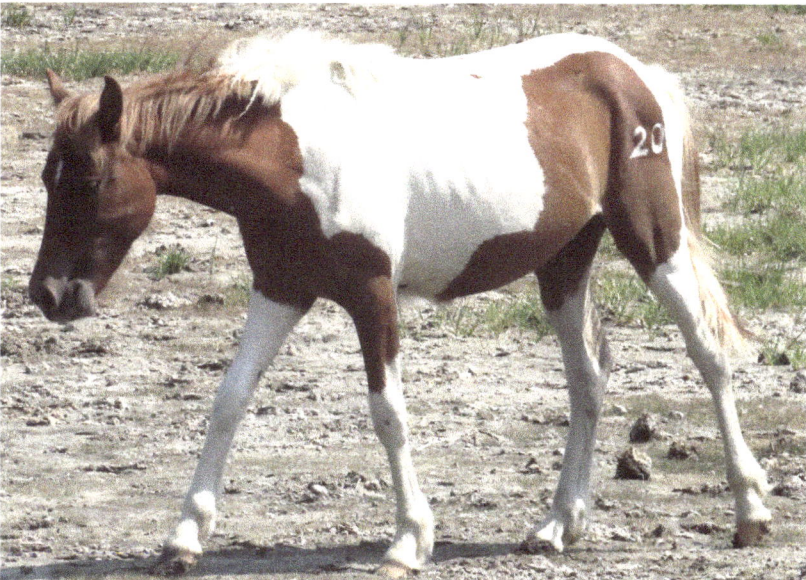

Chestnut Pinto

Courtney's Island Dove

Dove
mare   birth year: 2006   brand: unreadable
Courtney's Boy x Salt and Pepper

Brown eyes. Auction price: $2,300. Buyback donor: Joann Rome and Ginny Zlevitch.

Video Clip

Pedigree

Notes:

Courtney's Island Dove

Chestnut Pinto

Landis & RJ's Jubilation

Cottontail, Jubilation
mare   birth year: 2021   brand: 21
SURFER'S RIPTIDE x SONNY'S LEGACY

Brown eyes. Auction price: $11,900. First seen April 19, 2021.

Video Clip   Pedigree

Notes:

Landis & RJ's Jubilation

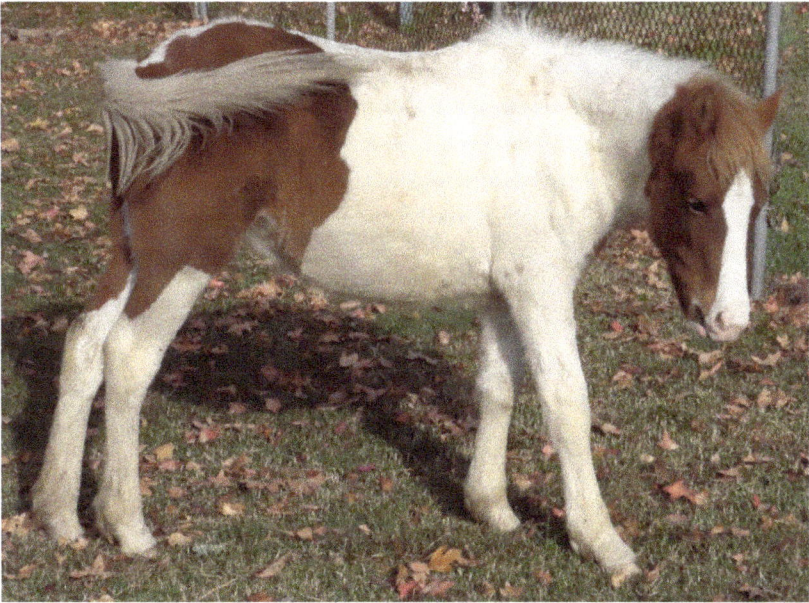

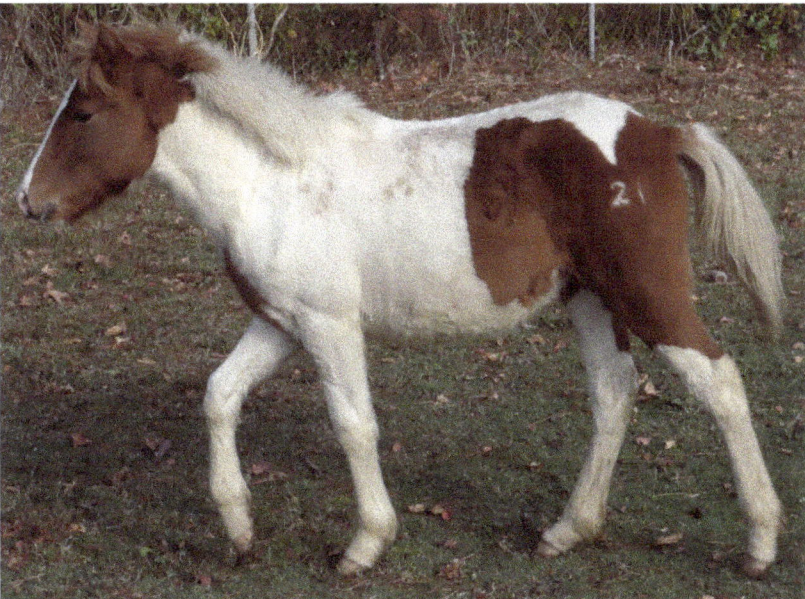

Chestnut Pinto

Little Bit O' Joansie

Joansie
mare   birth year: 2014   brand: 14
Courtney's Boy x Cinnamon Blaze

Brown eyes. Auction price: $7,100.

Video Clip

Pedigree

Notes:

_____

_____

_____

_____

_____

_____

_____

_____

Little Bit O' Joansie

Chestnut Pinto

Cher's Hope

Cher
mare   birth year: 2020   brand: 20
Tornado's Prince of Tides x Catwalk Chaos

Brown eyes. Auction price: $20,250. First seen March 29, 2020. Buyback donor: Cheryl Kornegay.

Video Clip

Pedigree

Notes:

Cher's Hope

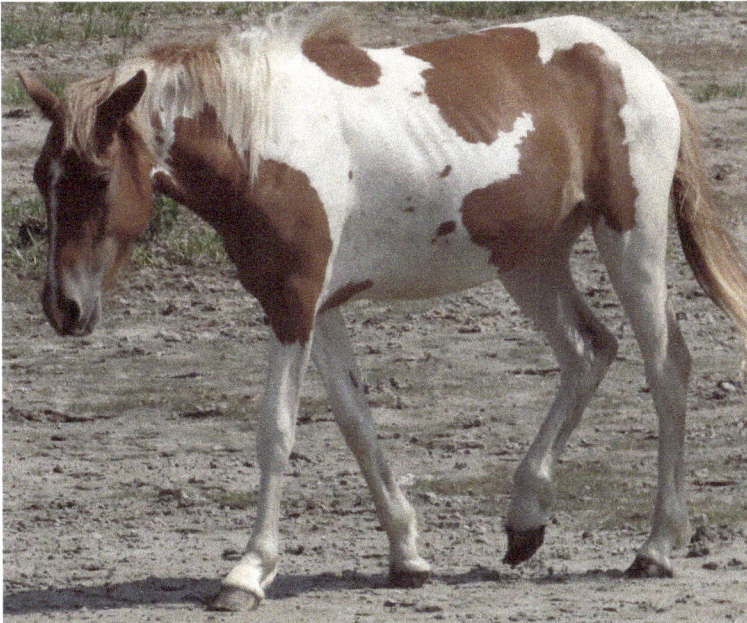

Chestnut Pinto

Don Leonard Stud II

Lenny, Leonard Stud II
stallion   birth year: 2014   brand: 14
PHANTOM MIST X TUNIE

Brown eyes. Auction price: $9,000. Buyback donor: Leonard Family.

Video Clip   Pedigree

Notes:

Don Leonard Stud II

Chestnut Pinto

Mary Read

mare   birth year: 2017   brand: 17
TORNADO'S LEGACY x ANNE BONNY

Brown eyes. Auction price: $7,500. First seen March 5, 2017. Buyback donator: Darcy Cole, Allison Dotzel, and Sarah Sickles.

Notes:

_____

_____

_____

_____

_____

_____

_____

_____

Mary Read

Chestnut Pinto

Thetis

mare   birth year: 2001   brand: 01
HOT AIR BALLOON x UNTOUCHABLE

Brown eyes. Born July 19, 2001. Alternate sire: Courtney's Boy.

Video Clip

Pedigree

Notes:

Thetis

Chestnut Pinto

Sonny's Legacy

mare   birth year: 2013   brand: 13
Don Leonard Stud x Shy Anne

Brown eyes. Born May 10, 2013. Not auctioned, donated in memory of fireman Sonny Haigh.

Video Clip

Pedigree

Notes:

Sonny's Legacy

Chestnut Pinto

Gidget's Beach Baby

Beach Baby
mare   birth year: 2010   brand: none
NORTH STAR x SURFER DUDE'S GIDGET

Brown eyes. Auction price: $5,500. Born May 13, 2010. Buyback donator: Buyback Babes.

Video Clip

Pedigree

Notes:

Gidget's Beach Baby

Chestnut Pinto

Wildfire

mare   birth year: 2013   brand: none
WH NIGHTWIND x WH SEA BREEZE

Brown eyes. Donated to CVFC March 2018. Great Great Great Grandfoal of Misty.

Video Clip

Pedigree

Notes:

Chestnut Pinto

Wildfire

Chestnut Pinto

Casade's Fancy Pants

Fancy Pants
mare   birth year: 2020   brand: 20
SURFER'S RIPTIDE x POCO'S STARRY NIGHT

Brown eyes. Auction price: $11,500. First seen May 16, 2020. Buyback donor: Toni Cox.

Video Clip   Pedigree

Notes:

Casade's Fancy Pants

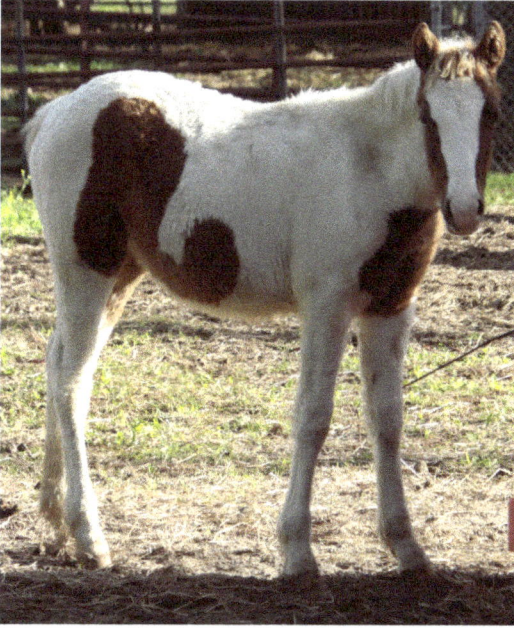

Chestnut Pinto

Thunderstorm Skies

Thunder
mare   birth year: 2013   brand: 13
DON LEONARD STUD x LILY PAD

Brown eyes. Auction price: $4,000. Born May 7, 2013. Buyback donator: Laura and George De Berdt Romilly.

Video Clip

Pedigree

Notes:

Thunderstorm Skies

Chestnut Pinto

CLG Rumor Has It

Rumor
mare   birth year: 2018   brand: 18
KEN x WHISPER OF LIVING LEGEND

One blue eye, one brown eye. Auction price: $13,200. First seen May 9, 2018. Buyback donor: Chincoteague Legacy Group.

Video Clip   Pedigree

Notes:

Chestnut Pinto

CLG Rumor Has It

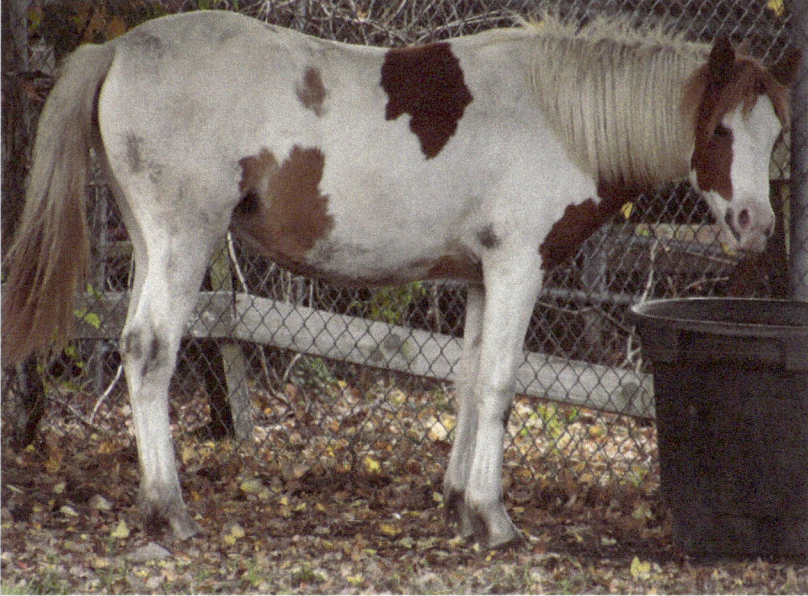

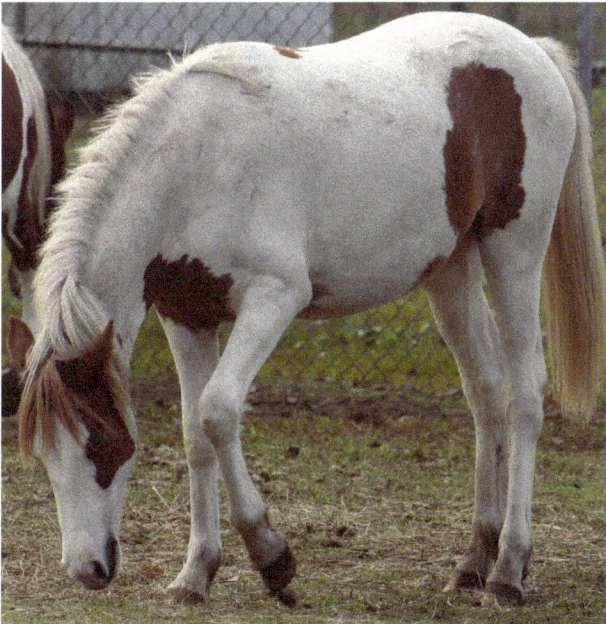

Chestnut Pinto

Delilah's Sandpiper

Piper
mare   birth year: 2020   brand: 20
CLG ToMorrow's Tidewater Twist x MissMe

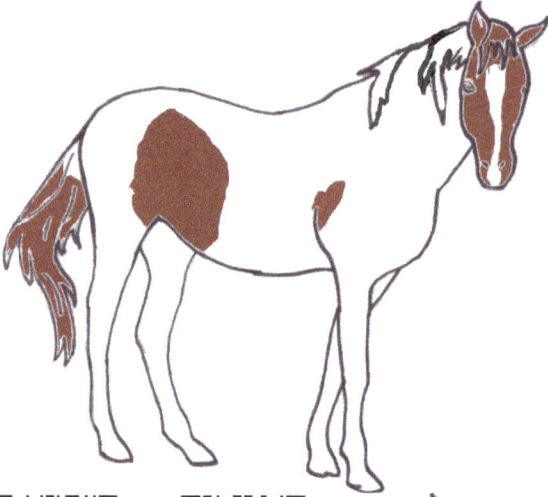

Brown eyes. Auction
price: $14,800. First
seen May 21, 2020.
Buyback donor: Judy
Fuccello.

Notes:

Delilah's Sandpiper

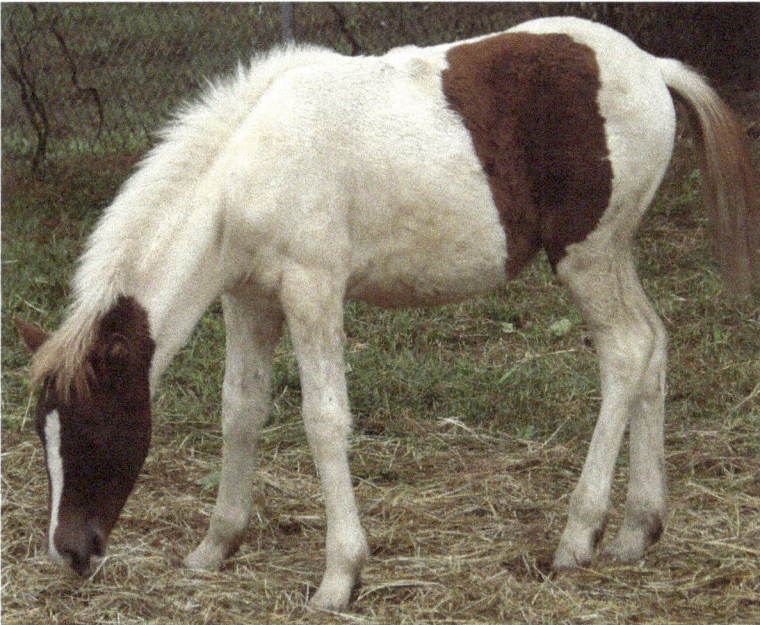

Palomino

Chief Golden Eagle

Chief
stallion   birth year: 2008   brand: 08
GLACIER x BEAUTIFUL DREAMER

Brown eyes. Auction price: $3,800. Born April 1, 2008. Buyback donor: Joann Rome and Ginny Zlevitch.

Video Clip   Pedigree

Notes:

Chief Golden Eagle

Palomino

Kachina Mayli Mist

Mayli
mare   birth year: 2012   brand: 12
PHANTOM MIST x KACHINA GRAND STAR

Brown eyes. Auction price: $7,000. Born April 3, 2012. Buyback donator: Joanne Rome, Ginny Zelevitch, Lowery Family.

Video Clip

Pedigree

Notes:

Palomino

Kachina Mayli Mist

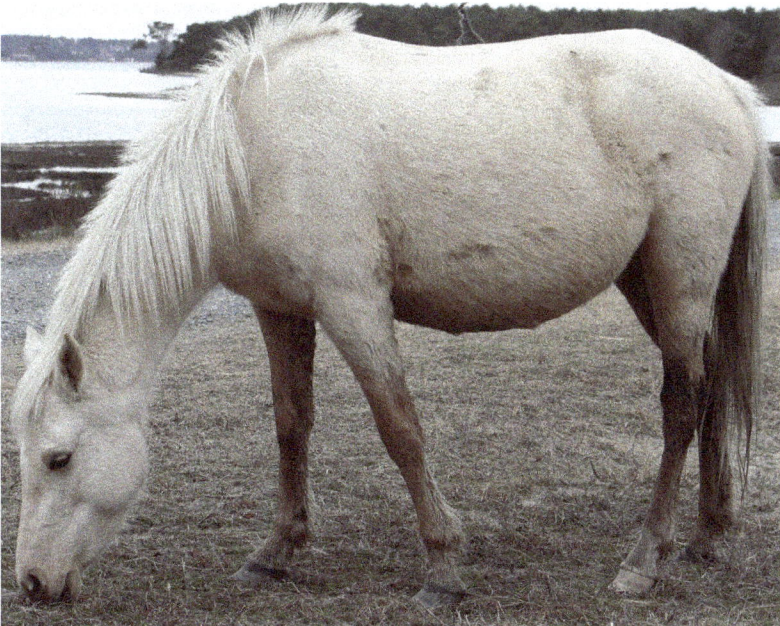

Palomino

Shy & Sassy Sweet Lady Suede

Suede
mare   birth year: 2014   brand: 14
CHIEF GOLDEN EAGLE x PONY LADIES' SWEET SURPRISE

Brown eyes. Auction price: $7,000. Buyback donator: Kim Theriault.

 Video Clip  Pedigree

Notes:

_____

_____

_____

_____

_____

_____

_____

_____

Palomino

Shy & Sassy Sweet Lady Suede

Palomino

Two Teague's Golden Girl

Goldie
mare   birth year: 2016   brand: 16
CHIEF GOLDEN EAGLE x TWO TEAGUES TACO

Brown eyes. Auction price: $5,000. First seen May 14, 2016. Buyback donator: Buyback Babes.

Video Clip

Pedigree

Notes:

Two Teague's Golden Girl

Palomino

Miss Admiral Halsey

mare   birth year: 2018   brand: 18
Surfer's Riptide x Kachina Mayli Mist

Brown eyes. Auction price: $10,200. First seen May 1, 2018. Buyback donator: Meredith Wright.

Notes:

Miss Admiral Halsey

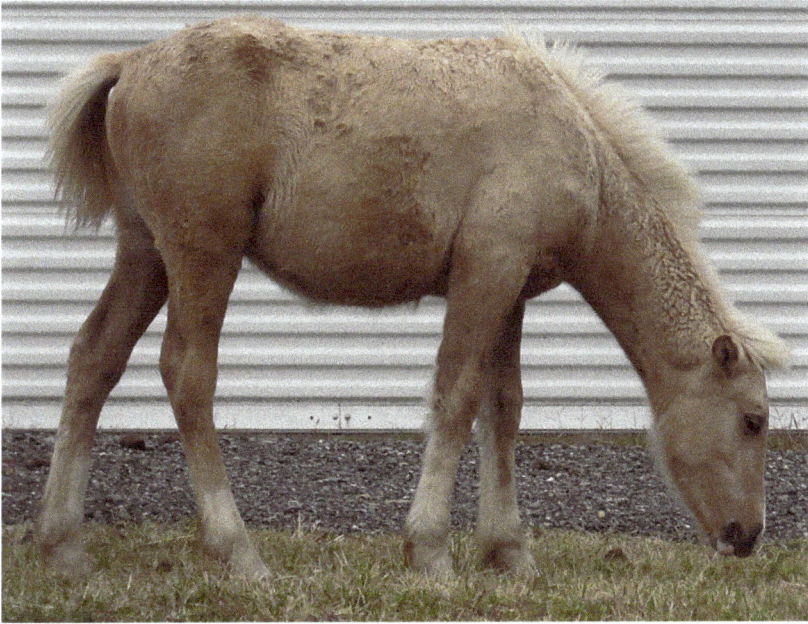

Palomino Comparison Chart

Name	Pg #	Brand	Mane	Face
Chief Golden Eagle	294	08	left	
Kachina Mayli Mist	296	12	left	
Miss Admiral Halsey	302	18	left	blaze
Shy & Sassy Sweet Lady Suede	298	14	split	
Two Teague's Golden Girl	300	16	left	

NOTES

Left & right refers to the animal's left & right.

Mane: left = falls to the left **right** = falls to the right **split** = significant portion falls on left and right

Legs				Notable Details
R F	**R B**	**L F**	**L B**	
				stallion; long forelock
				pale coat; short hairs stand up along neck like a mohawk
sock	sock	sock	sock	only one with white on face and legs

R F = right front   **R B** = right back **L F** = left front   **L B** = left back
sock = white well below the knee   **stocking** = white near and above the knee

baldface = white covers most of the face   **blaze** = white streak running down the length of the face   **snip** = white spot on the muzzle   **star** = white spot on the forehead

Palomino Pinto

Judy's Sunshine

Wings
mare   birth year: 2018   brand: 18
TORNADO'S PRINCE OF TIDES x CATWALK CHAOS

Brown eyes. Auction price: $20,000. First seen March 5, 2018. Buyback donor: Judy Ann White.

Video Clip

Pedigree

Notes:

Judy's Sunshine

Palomino Pinto

Tornado's Prince of Tides

Prince
stallion   birth year: 2007   brand: 07
Tornado x Sand Cherry

Brown eyes. Auction price: $17,500. Born April 7, 2007. Buyback donator: Buyback Babes.

Video Clip   Pedigree

Notes:

_____

_____

_____

_____

_____

_____

_____

_____

Tornado's Prince of Tides

Palomino Pinto

Mz Peg

Peggy
mare   birth year: 2020   brand: 20
Tornado's Legacy x White Saddle

Brown eyes. Auction
price: $25,000. First
seen May 12, 2020.
Buyback donor: George
Panos in memory of
Peggy McWhirt.

Video Clip   Pedigree

Notes:

Mz Peg

Palomino Pinto

Little Miss Sunshine

Sunshine
mare   birth year: 2015   brand: 15
Tornado's Prince of Tides x Baybe

Brown eyes. Auction price: $5,300. Born July 3, 2015. Buyback donor: Joanne Niland and Nancie Oleynik.

Video Clip

Pedigree

Notes:

Little Miss Sunshine

Palomino Pinto

Jigsaw's Little Miss Skeeter

Skeeter
mare   birth year: 2018   brand: 18
Tornado's Legacy x Cody's Little Jigsaw Puzzle

Brown eyes. Auction price: $11,500. First seen May 4, 2018.

Video Clip

Pedigree

Notes:

_____

_____

_____

_____

_____

_____

_____

_____

_____

Jigsaw's Little Miss Skeeter

Palomino Pinto

SCC Misty's Sunburst

Sunburst
mare   birth year: 2021   brand: 21
DON LEONARD STUD II x SUNDANCE

Brown eyes. Auction price: $21,250. First seen April 24, 2021. Great Great Great Great Grandfoal of Misty. Buyback donor: Stoney Creek Chincoteagues.

Video Clip

Pedigree

Notes:

SCC Misty's Sunburst

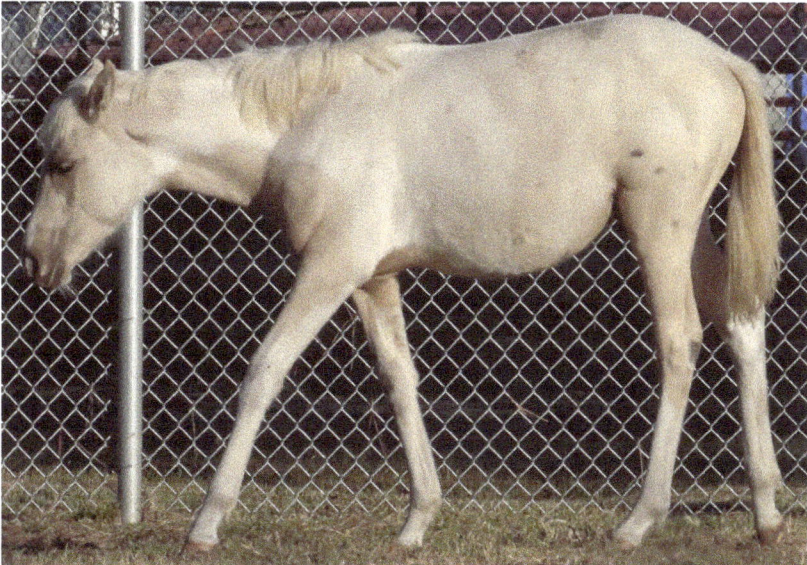

Palomino Pinto

Marina's Marsh Mallow

Marsh Mallow
mare   birth year: 2014   brand: 14
Tornado's Prince of Tides x Fifteen Friends of Freckles

Brown eyes. Auction
price: $7,000. Buyback
donator: Cassou
family.

Video Clip   Pedigree

Notes:

Marina's Marsh Mallow

Palomino Pinto

Lorna Dune

mare   birth year: 2013   brand: 13
Don Leonard Stud x Jessica's Sea Star Sandy

Brown eyes. Auction price: $6,200. Born May 5, 2013. Buyback donator: Kathleen Cahall.

Video Clip   Pedigree

Notes:

Palomino Pinto

Lorna Dune

Close Family Index

In order to save space, the relationship of an entry in this index is identified by font and color.

Color Key

Name - Bold Black
SIRE - Small Caps Blue
DAM - Small Caps Pink
Offspring - Green
Sibling Same Sire - Italics Blue
Sibling Same Dam - Italics Pink
Sibling Same Sire & Dam - Italics Black

A Splash of Freckles, 106
FIFTEEN FRIENDS OF FRECKLES, 92 CLG Magic Moment, 140 Good Golly Miss Molly, 38 *Archer's Gambit*, 256 *CJ SAMM'N*, 230 *Fifteen Friends of Freckles*, 92 *Gidget's Beach Baby*, 282 *Heide's Sky*, 112 *Kachina Grand Star*, 160 *Kimball's Rainbow Delight*, 232 *Little Duckie*, 248 *Marina's Marsh Mallow*, 318 *Myrt & Brenda's Indiana Girl*, 260

Ace's Black Tie Affair, 128
Ace's Miss Raven Rhapsody, 126 Carli Marie, 242 Shelley's Shell Search, 132 Two Teagues Taco's Chilibean, 250

Ace's Miss Raven Rhapsody, 126
ACE'S BLACK TIE AFFAIR, 128 MARINA'S MARSH MALLOW, 318 *Carli Marie*, 242 *Shelley's Shell Search*, 132 *Two Teagues Taco's Chilibean*, 250

Ajax, 60
Catwalk's Olympic Glory, 226 MissMe, 62 Rosie's Teapot, 32 Sky Dancer, 100 *Anne Bonny*, 244 *Ella of Assateague*, 44 *Molly's Rosebud*, 164 *Skylark*, 94

Amari's Journey, 42
DON LEONARD STUD II, 274 RANDY, 178 *SCC Misty's Sunburst*, 316

Anne Bonny, 244
Anne Bonny's Little Flower, 144 Mary Read, 276 *Ajax*, 60 *Molly's Rosebud*, 164

Anne Bonny's Little Flower, 144
TORNADO'S LEGACY, 174 ANNE BONNY, 244 *Clara's Glory*, 264 *CLG Magic Moment*, 140 *CLG Rider on the Storm*, 146 *CLG ToMorrow's Tidewater Twist*, 170 *Good Golly Miss Molly*, 38 *Jigsaw's Little Miss Skeeter*, 314 *Loughlin's Luck of the Irish*, 168 *Marguerite of Chincoteague*, 88 ***Mary Read***, 276 *Mz Peg*, 310

Close Family Index

Close Family Index

Close Family Index

Close Family Index

Close Family Index

Close Family Index

Little Duckie, 248
SWEET JANE, 246 *A Splash of Freckles*, 106 *Archer's Gambit*, 256 *Beach Bunny*, 254 *CJ SAMM'N*, 230 *Fifteen Friends of Freckles*, 92 *Gidget's Beach Baby*, 282 *Kachina Grand Star*, 160 *Kimball's Rainbow Delight*, 232

Little Miss Sunshine, 312
TORNADO'S PRINCE OF TIDES, 308 BAYBE, 138 *Badabing*, 172 *Cher's Hope*, 272 **CLG Bay Princess**, 166 *Judy's Sunshine*, 306 *Marina's Marsh Mallow*, 318 **Randy**, 178

Liz's Serenity, 154
Fancy Free, 148 *Little Dolphin*, 12 *Sweetheart*, 68

Lorna Dune, 320
JESSICA'S SEA STAR SANDY, 152 *Ivana Marie Zustan*, 150 *Poco's Starry Night*, 130 *Sonny's Legacy*, 280 *Sunrise Ocean Tides*, 158 *Thunderstorm Skies*, 288

Loughlin's Luck of the Irish, 168
TORNADO'S LEGACY, 174 TIGER LILY, 236 *Anne Bonny's Little Flower*, 144 *Clara's Glory*, 264 *CLG Magic Moment*, 140 *CLG Rider on the Storm*, 146 *CLG ToMorrow's Tidewater Twist*, 170 *Good Golly Miss Molly*, 38 *Jigsaw's Little Miss Skeeter*, 314 *Marguerite of Chincoteague*, 88 *Mary Read*, 276 *Mz Peg*, 310

Loveland's Secret Feather, 80
WILD THING, 82 *Beau of Artemis*, 76 *CLG Pennies From Heaven*, 204 *Splash*, 74 *Doctor Amrien*, 48 **Grandma's Dream**, 78 *Henry's Hidalgo*, 70 *Ken*, 218 *Maverick*, 108 *Skylark*, 94

Marguerite of Chincoteague, 88
TORNADO'S LEGACY, 174 MIRACLE'S NATURAL BEAUTY, 52 *Anne Bonny's Little Flower*, 144 *Clara's Glory*, 264 *CLG Magic Moment*, 140 **CLG Rider on the Storm**, 146 *CLG ToMorrow's Tidewater Twist*, 170 *Good Golly Miss Molly*, 38 *Jigsaw's Little Miss Skeeter*, 314 *Loughlin's Luck of the Irish*, 168 *Mary Read*, 276 *MissMe*, 62 *Mz Peg*, 310

Marina's Marsh Mallow, 318
TORNADO'S PRINCE OF TIDES, 308 FIFTEEN FRIENDS OF FRECKLES, 92 Ace's Miss Raven Rhapsody, 126 *A Splash of Freckles*, 106 *Badabing*, 172 *Cher's Hope*, 272 *CLG Bay Princess*, 166 *Heide's Sky*, 112 *Judy's Sunshine*, 306 *Little Miss Sunshine*, 312 *Myrt & Brenda's Indiana Girl*, 260 *Randy*, 178

Mary Read, 276
TORNADO'S LEGACY, 174 ANNE BONNY, 244 Captain Carlton's Martha Lou, 72 **Anne Bonny's Little Flower**, 144 *Clara's Glory*, 264 *CLG Magic Moment*, 140 *CLG Rider on the Storm*, 146 *CLG ToMorrow's Tidewater Twist*, 170 *Good Golly Miss Molly*, 38 *Jigsaw's Little Miss Skeeter*, 314 *Loughlin's Luck of the Irish*, 168 *Marguerite of Chincoteague*, 88 *Mz Peg*, 310

Close Family Index

Close Family Index

Close Family Index

334

Stallion Index

Brand Index

Brand Index

www.ingramcontent.com/pod-product-compliance
Lightning Source LLC
Chambersburg PA
CBHW041254040426
42334CB00028BA/3015